D1506728

SOMETHING TO PROVE

Something to Prove

Revised Edition

SOMETHING TO PROVE

Ann Cole Lowe

Praise for Something to Prove

"Until recently, Black women's accomplishments have not been given enough appreciation. The thought that Black fashion designers even exist still shocks many people. To right this wrong, it's important to go back through fashion history and retrieve the names of those designers who have been overlooked and uplift that name. Julia Faye Smith's book, *Something to Prove* presents an important first step in uplifting fashion designer Ann Lowe's name. There is much love for Ann Lowe and her artistry in pages along with full appreciation for Lowe's amazing work in fashion. Smith's words represent an important first step toward the complete embrace of Lowe and the journey to recover her art to put her firmly in the art world where she belongs. Something to Prove proves that a Black woman born in rural Clayton, Alabama deserves a place among the best fashion designers. One day, God willing, because of efforts like Smith's, Ann Lowe will be there."

Dr. Piper Huguley, author of By Design: the story of Ann Lowe, Society's Best-Kept Secret.
A historical fiction publishing in 2022

Dedicated to the memory of my mother,
Myrtie Rice Dockery McJenkins,
who had her own personal style,

And
to the current fashion leaders of the family,
both male and female:
skajejl

Something to Prove

A Biography of Ann Cole Lowe
America's Forgotten Fashion Designer

Julia Faye Dockery Smith

ISBN: 13: 978-1532981333
ISBN: 10: 1532981333
Paperback

Something to Prove: Ann Cole Lowe/Julia Faye Dockery
Smith
Includes bibliographical references
Cataloging data: Ann Cole Lowe, Ann Lowe, African
American Women, Fashion, Fashion Design, African
American Fashion Design, African American Fashion
Designer, Alabama, Clayton, Montgomery, Tampa, New
York, Mrs. Emmett O'Neal, Ak-Sar-Ben, Gasparilla, ,
Jacqueline Bouvier Kennedy, Marjorie Merriweather Post,
Olivia de Havilland, Strong Women

NOTE

To view the photos found in this book and more go to
https://www.pinterest.com/juliafsmith7/something-to-
prove/

Table of Contents

FRONTMATTER

PART I: The South
Alabama and Florida

PART II: New York and Beyond
New York and Paris

PART III: The Most Photographed

Wedding Dress In American History

PART IV: Ann's Studio
Creating Magic

PART V: Remembering Ann

PART VI:
Miscellaneous, Afterthoughts
Museums, Inconsistencies, About the author,
NOTE:
As you read, you might want to picture an actress or actor playing certain parts of Ann's life for I have sold the film rights to a Hollywood producer and the theatrical rights to a company in Great Britain. They are developing the story as a musical. I wonder who you would choose to play the various people in Ann's life. 9/2021

Ann's Personal Style

While Ann was creating for others, she was also developing and enhancing her own style. The following three photographs show Ann's simple, elegant style that easily identified her as a woman of taste. The sophisticated simplicity was reminiscent of other fashionable women and designers. The signature hat was added because, as Ann put it, "my hair was thinning."

Photo of Ann courtesy of Clara C. Harvey,
Great-granddaughter of Ann Cole Lowe

"Some of the pictures that you see, of Chanel, I...I think of Ann Lowe, that sort of simple elegant, with different coloured skin, but a lady beautifully dressed with a hat, who was making clothes."
Betty King, Debutant

Photo courtesy Wikipedia Commons, fair use

Ann Cole Lowe

Photo courtesy of Clara C. Harvey, Great-granddaughter of Ann Cole Lowe.

There was, however, more to her style than vanity. She knew for whom she wanted to design and sew, and she consciously dressed to tell that world that she could not only create style but that she was a stylish lady herself. She knew that her appearance went a long way in achieving success.

"I feel so happy when I am making clothes that I could just jump up and down with joy."

Ann Lowe, Oakland Tribune

Ann's Professional Style

This wonderful example of Ann's work has been lost and is not in any museum. Thank you to the lucky young lady who owned it for sharing this photo of a lost Ann Lowe gem. *Photo Courtesy of Patricia Penrose (Schieffer).*

While Ann's personal style was simple with muted colors, her professional designs were quite the opposite. Even though Ann always worked with her clients to provide what the client wanted, Ann's preference for certain design elements can be found throughout her body of work.

As one views examples of Ann's designs, there are certain hallmarks, both visible and invisible to the naked eye, often found in most of her creations. Ann liked 'portrait' necklines, capped sleeves, big skirts, fine fabrics, and floral embellishments everywhere. Equally important were the interior finished seams, structure to add body, and undergarment supports.

The exquisite white silk faille with white silk roses and leaves with rhinestones on the following page exemplifies many of Ann's design hallmarks, both exterior and interior. One can readily see the wide portrait neckline with built-in cap sleeves, the voluminous skirt, and the 3-D hand-made flowers that blend in beautifully with Ms. Penrose's bouquet. The photo epitomizes Ann's gift for design and sewing. The gown, worn by Patricia Penrose (Schieffer) at the Assembly Ball November 1959 in Fort Worth, Texas, was purchased it from the Adam Room of Saks Fifth Avenue.

See two other Ann Lowe gowns worn by Ms. Penrose in PART IV, Portfolio II.)

Something to Prove

"Deep in every heart, slumbers a dream"

Christian Dior

PART I: THE SOUTH
ALABAMA AND FLORIDA

Introduction

"You ask me where's home? Well, I'll tell you. It's wherever I am sewing and designing. Still, there's one special place that is home in my heart. It's the place where I learned to design and sew and love flowers.

As a child, I enjoyed playing in the sewing room of my Mama and Grandmama's house. It was a place strewn with scraps of beautiful fabrics---light as silky sunshine in the summer and heavy as a warm blanket in the winter.

That's how I learned about the seasons and the flowers. Colorful roses, azaleas, dogwoods, and zinnias meant summer; poinsettias, hollies, and holiday cactus mean winter. Between those seasons we had daffodils and primroses in the spring and chrysanthemums and apple blossoms in the fall.

Those flowers mean home to me. Those flowers found their way from the long summer and short winter days into the heart of my mind. With scraps from the sewing room fabrics, my brain guided my hands and with patience, I learned to create those lovely flowers of home. So no matter where life was to take me, that part of 'home' was always with me."

Chapter 1: Background

In the last decade of the 19th Century, seventy-seven miles southwest of Montgomery, Alabama, a baby girl was born. Named Ann, she changed fashion history forever, but as the sun rose on the morning of Ann's birth, no one in the small town of Clayton, Alabama could have dreamed of the heights she would achieve for she was born a squirming, scrawny, little Black girl in the Jim Crow South.

Her path would not be easy, and any dreams she might have were certain to be achieved only with great determination and fortitude on her part. Those qualities she had in abundance, paired with talent and ambition. Her dreams were unlikely dreams, but Ann would, from an early age, recognize them and strive to achieve them.

Ann knew her background and that of her culture presented obstacles, but as always when she thought about the obstacles, she armed herself with a great inner strength which combined with a natural talent that came from the women of her family who had gone before her. So fortified, she knew she could rise above all obstacles and forge her own future.

In the early 1800s divisive political and economic ideologies were evident within the United States of America. The South, the states south of the Mason Dixon Line and the Ohio River, was largely agricultural with a long growing season, a plantation system of slave labor, small individually owned farms, and a belief in a state's right to determine for itself the way of life within its borders.

The North, states above the Mason Dixon Line and the Ohio River and further to the west, was a more industrialized society with a belief in a strong central government that overrode the individual rights of states on certain matters.

By the mid-1840s, these economic, political, and cultural divisions were becoming more apparent with each passing year. The debate over slavery was the most divisive issue of the era. Most southerners spoke loudly in support of slavery. Most northerners did not. The abolitionist movement, the movement to do away with slavery, was increasing in the North. This development worried the southern plantation owners. Still, they clung to their opinions and their way of life which depended upon slavery.

The growth of slavery in the southern state of Georgia propelled it to be the home of more slaves and slaveholders than any other state in the Lower South. By the end of the antebellum era, Georgia was second only to Virginia among all slaveholding states. At the beginning of the decade, the slave population was 280,944 and growing. Georgia's slave population is important to our story for it is there that we catch the first recognizable threads of Ann's story-- long before her birth.

To know Ann's story it is important is understand the role of women in the slave community. Within that community, slave women were subordinate not only because of their race but also because of their gender. Women slaves worked in two distinct areas: fieldwork where they performed primarily unskilled agricultural tasks and domestic work, within the structure of the household. A skilled seamstress would be a member of the latter division of labor and on a plantation deep in the heart of the South, she would be an important part of plantation life.

It was within the domestic culture of seamstresses that members of the sisterhood of female slavery were able to show their artistic ability as well as their skill. In addition to the seamstresses themselves, the women who spun the yarn and those who wove the yarn into cloth might also benefit from their artistic abilities. One of the benefits sometimes associated with these skilled positions, especially for the seamstresses, was increased respect among fellow slaves and their masters. There are records of skilled slaves seamstresses earning widespread respect and sometimes deferential terms of address. In addition, skilled seamstress slaves sometimes benefited from cash payments if their owners allowed them to work for others for wages. If their owners allowed them to keep all or part of those wages earned, the seamstresses might someday hope to purchase their freedom.

On a Georgia plantation owned by a Tompkins family, there lived one of those talented slave seamstresses. She was skilled with her needle and had an eye for design. Her expert services were in demand for everything from family ball gowns to work garments for the slaves.

It was into that setting in approximately 1844 that Georgia Tompkins, identified by her heritage as a mulatto slave, was born. She was the daughter of the plantation owner and his wife's skilled, but unnamed in historical records, seamstress slave. Even though the father of the baby was the master of the plantation, the baby girl would as the law mandated, be a slave from birth. Baby Georgia was to become Ann's Grandmother.

During the 1800s, slaves were not the only members of the Negro race living in the South during the 1800s. By 1860, the year of Lincoln's first election, 488,070 free Blacks were living in the United States. Of this total, 261,918 lived in the South. In other words, 35,766 more free Blacks lived in the Southern slave-owning states than in the Northern states.

Free Blacks living in the North in the antebellum period were quite outspoken in their opposition to slavery. Free Blacks living in the South during this time lived under the shadow of slavery. These Southern Free Men of Color had a slight advantage over the slaves because they could usually live and work where they desired, but they still faced restrictions from laws and society. They were forced to carry their papers proving their free state; without these papers, they were subject to capture. Their everyday lives were impacted for even though they could gather together in churches, schools, and social organizations, these gatherings brought intense scrutiny by the establishment.

A number of free Blacks owned slaves. It has been reported that 26 percent of the free Blacks in Alabama and 20 percent of the free Blacks in Georgia's home state of Georgia were slave owners. Why were free Blacks willing to own others? There were those, of course, who were willing to own anyone who would do their work for them, but this is not generally accepted as the major reason for free Blacks owning members of their own race.

Many of the slaves purchased by free Blacks were relatives whom they later manumitted, or freed, or depending on the local laws, kept enslaved for their, the slaves', own safety. In some states, when a slave owner freed a slave, that slave was forced, by law, to leave the state. If a free man of color purchased a slave and made her his wife, he would probably not want to free her and have her forced to leave the state they were residing in as husband and wife. If he did not free his wife, as many such husbands failed to do, his own children of that union were born his slaves and were thus reported to the slave counters as slaves.

Chapter 2: The Family

Grandmama, Georgia Tompkins

There is no definitive history of Georgia's life on the plantation during her childhood. Our twentieth and twenty-first century generations have read of both kindnesses and atrocities, even to the acknowledged mulattoes with ties to the white males of the plantations. Was she acknowledged to be a daughter of the plantation throughout her life? Was she favored? Was she mistreated? Under what conditions did Georgia live and grow? We simply don't know. We know that as an adult her parentage was acknowledged and she is listed in records as a Tompkins and as a mulatto. By definition, a mulatto is someone born from one Black parent and one white parent or to someone born of two mulatto parents.

Nothing is known of Georgia's mother and father's relationship. Was it forced? Was it not? Was it ongoing? Brief? An older male sibling is also listed in the census record as a mulatto while younger brothers and sisters are listed as Negro. Records do not give the details of the older brother's parentage.

From her seamstress mother, Georgia learned to sew with such skill that she joined her mother in the big house, doing housekeeping chores and sewing for the white family. During this antebellum period, the seamstresses of the plantation homes were in great demand as fancy dresses were elaborate and time-consuming to make. Since sewing machines were in their infancy and not readily available, it can be assumed that some, if not all, sewing on a Southern plantation was still done by hand. One method of embellishment of these fancy gowns was through embroidery and Georgia became an excellent embroiderer.

This is the setting in which Georgia's skill with needle and thread grew. This is the setting in which Georgia's education, bequeathed by her mother and all the other unnamed seamstresses who went before her, began. It was also the setting for the legacy she bequeathed to her own daughters and eventually to her granddaughter Ann.

Grandpa, General Cole

In the year 1853 a young carpenter of twenty-three moved north from his hometown of Abbeville, Alabama to Clayton, Alabama, a distance of about thirty miles. His name was General Cole; he was a carpenter by trade, and he was a free man of color. The General in his name does not refer to a military title, but simply to the name given him by his parents. The name was later passed on to one of his sons. General's move to this small rural town allowed him to join the construction crew building the new Barbour County Courthouse. This move became the catalyst for his future family in Barbour County.

Barbour County Courthouse of 1853, built at a cost of $9,695.00. Photo courtesy of *http://courthousehistory.com/gallery/states/alabama/coun ties/barbour*

After completion of the courthouse, General's skills allowed him to remain and work on other carpentry projects. For years to come, General was part of the construction scene in Barbour County and surrounding areas. Barbour County is known for its beautiful antebellum homes; several of the historic homes in Barbour County could very possibly be part of General's resume. Perhaps he was part of the construction crew for the Miller-Martin townhouse pictured below.

Photo courtesy of *Rivers Langley SaveRivers* The **Miller-Martin Town House** a historic house in Clayton, Alabama, U.S.. built as a townhouse for John H. Miller in 1859. Designed in the Gothic Revival architectural style. It has been listed on the National Register of Historic Places since December 16, 1974.

Grandmama and Grandpa Cole

Sometime between 1853 and 1860 General Cole met Georgia and according to family history, he "fell in love with a her, purchased her from her owners, and married her, making her a free woman."

We do not know how or where they met. Perhaps her Georgia plantation owners had a second plantation in Alabama, perhaps she was visiting there with her owners, or perhaps General made a trip to Georgia and they actually met there. Georgia was approximately 16 years old and General was about 30 years when they made their first home in Alabama.

The question arises, did he free her immediately or did the uncertain setting of the time persuade him to keep ownership as a means of protecting her? Without the process of manumission, the legal act of a slave owner freeing his or her slaves, a slave who married a free person of color was still considered a slave. Records for the manumission of Georgia by General Cole cannot be found in either Georgia or Alabama. Did he free her immediately? Did he, perhaps, not free her at all, following the practice of many such unions, as a way to keep her safe from bounty hunters. Additionally, as his wife, he wanted to keep her with him. Many states, including Alabama, at one time or another forced freed slaves to move out of the state. Simply as his wife, even with legal papers of freedom, she may not have been as free and as safe as he wanted her to be. Thus, as his 'slave' she would have been safer and the family would be kept intact.

In either case, we know that, since Alabama did not cease supporting the Confederacy as required by the Emancipation Proclamation, she would have been freed by the Proclamation in January of 1863, but would she have felt free to assert her freedom? Finally, for all time, she and all other slaves were freed by the 13th Amendment to the Constitution when it was adopted in 1865.

Aside from the question of when Georgia became a free woman, a second question relating to the marriage of General Cole and Georgia is raised by the records of Barbour County and Alabama. The official marriage license for General Cole and Georgia Tompkins gives November 8, 1867 as their wedding date. Family history states that after purchasing her, General and Georgia married. Perhaps they had a church, family, cultural or private ceremony which tied them together as man and wife. We know that General and Georgia were living together as man and wife for several years before this official recorded document. The thought of a legal, by society's standards, ceremony years later might have been considered simply a formality by them. Perhaps to remove any question of the legitimacy of their union, they reaffirmed and registered their vows.

It appears that General, Georgia, and their growing Cole family lived and grew in Clayton throughout the Civil War years, the reconstruction period, and into the 20th Century. Even though Clayton was rural, poor, and isolated, it was there that General and Georgia worked to raise their family. The couple eventually had many children. Some records show eight children and others eleven. As with many families in the second half of the 19th Century, several of the children did not survive; this might account for the disparity in the records.

According to the 1880 census, the family was still living in Clayton, Barbour Co., Al. General, age 50, is listed as head of the household and is a self-employed carpenter. Georgia, age 36, worked as a housekeeper and seamstress. The surviving children at that time included Hugh born in 1863, then Jane in 1864. They were followed by Lenora, General G., Louis, Willie, and Tommie. Interspersed with these live births were the losses of other children. In future census records some of these children will have left the family home and new ones will have been added.

Barbour County, AL

What was this place where a free man of color would choose to remain, marry, and raise a family? It was rural, sparsely populated, and part of Alabama's Black Belt, so named for its dark rich soil. Its fertile, rolling landscape was well situated to agriculture. The productive land and soft seasonal weather patterns extended the growing season making it home to dozens of flourishing slave-owning plantations.

Plantations and small farms had not always dotted the landscape for before the arrival of plantation owners and yeoman farmers, this was Indian Territory. After the War of 1812 with its bloody battles in the region, contested land was finally ceded by the Creek Confederation to the U.S. by the Treaty of Cusetta in 1832. This included what is now Barbour County. However, the local Native American population had been largely removed two years earlier.

Barbour County is located in the southeast corner of Alabama, immediately west of the Chattahoochee River and the State of Georgia. The county is named for James Barbour, Virginia governor, U. S. Senator and Secretary of War. It was Barbour who, as Secretary of War, successfully negotiated the removal of the Creek Nation from Alabama and Georgia. It was he who first proposed the creation of an Indian Territory west of the Mississippi.

Clayton became the county seat in 1834. It is located in the geographic center of the county on the headwaters of the Pea and the Choctawhatchee rivers. The town was named for Augustine Clayton, a Georgia judge and congressman.

14

The first courthouse was a log cabin. The population was small and even by the 1850s when General Cole moved to the area, the population of Clayton was still hovering around 500 people. The town and the county were, however, growing and a new courthouse was needed. General Cole's carpentry skills allowed him to be a part of this growth.

In the early years, Clayton supported several commercial venues including a number of dry goods stores and a dedicated rail system as part of the Central Railroad of Georgia.

Unfortunately, Clayton had a rival ---the nearby city of Eufaula, just twenty-one miles east of Clayton. Located on the banks of the Chattahoochee River, the natural boundary between Alabama and Georgia, Eufaula became an important shipping and commercial center. As money poured into Eufaula , it grew and prospered while Clayton to the southwest faltered.

Soon the citizens of Eufaula began lobbying to move the county seat from Clayton to Eufaula. Clayton fought back. The result was a compromise and both cities were awarded courthouses. Legal and criminal matters from the western half of the county would be settled in Clayton while legal and criminal matters from the eastern part of the county would be handled in Eufaula. This unconventional county government design still exists today. The 1853 Clayton courthouse no longer stands, replaced by a new one in 1961.

Alabama showing the location of Barbour County.

Today finds Clayton still rural, and still small. The town is not prosperous and while it is still part of Alabama's Black Belt, the fields of plantation era crops have largely disappeared. In their place, however, are lovely rolling hills of green grazing land, painting a bucolic scene of serenity.

The Cole Family After Slavery

Throughout the South, life was hard during the years of the Civil War and Reconstruction, but it has been said that the Cole family was better off than most Black families and many of their white neighbors. General Cole's carpentry skills, along with Georgia's work as a housekeeper and seamstress, enabled them to support their family. I never found evidence that the Cole women worked in the fields. At some point General Cole built a new home for his family within the 'town' limits of Clayton; they were townspeople in a rural area.

Around 1900, the Cole family moved to Montgomery. AL. General and Georgia were together from 1860 until 1907 when, in his seventies, General died. He, along with many other members of his family, is buried in the Pioneer Black Cemetery in Clayton.

Mama, Jane Cole Lowe, 186?-1914

Jane, the second of Georgia and General's children was Ann's mother. Jane, or Janie as she was called by the family, spent her growing and learning years in Clayton. Any formal schooling Janie received would have come from the segregated Freedman's Bureau schools of the Eufaula-Clayton district and no records for her have been found.

Even so, she grew up with her large family surrounding her and the women of the family were educating her in their own way. She was expected to learn a trade and become a contributing member of the household. Learning from these talented women, especially her mother Georgia, she became a skilled seamstress and embroiderer. In all likelihood, she probably designed many of her creations as her mother had done before her and as her daughter Ann would do after her.

Sometime before the early 1890s Jane married Jack Lowe. Little is known about Mr. Lowe other than his name. Their first child was a daughter. They named her Sallie, and she was their only child for several years. Sallie was light-skinned, showing her mixed heritage much more than her future little sister would. That little sister, the Lowe's second child, was born in the 1890s. Named Ann Cole Lowe, she was soon called Annie by the family.

Ann Cole Lowe 1898-1981

When Ann was born to Jane and Jack Lowe in the late 1900s, Clayton was still reinventing itself after the years of destruction and loss of the American Civil War. The population fluctuated between 1,000 and 2,000 people, most of them Black, most of them farmers adjusting to a new type of rural living. The fertile soil of Alabama's Black Belt was still available, thus keeping agriculture as the main source of income; it was simply being farmed differently. These farmers, both Black and white alike, worked long, hard hours trying to piece together a new life as sharecroppers and tenant farmers. As children were born into these families, they were expected to take their place alongside their elders in the fields. Again, I never found evidence that the Lowe sisters worked in the fields.

In the early 1900s, we don't know exactly when because of the discrepancy in records, the Cole and Lowe families moved from Clayton to Montgomery, Alabama, some seventy-four miles northwest of Clayton. Traveling by wagon over the rolling hills of south-central Alabama, the trip would have taken several days.

We also don't know why General and Georgia Cole along with Jack and Jane Lowe and their two daughters left Clayton, but reasons might be found in the prosperity and growth of the two areas in the late 1800s and the early 1900s. Montgomery was growing, Clayton was not. Montgomery was prospering, Clayton was not. Perhaps both Jack and Janie saw reason to leave the community she had always known but we have no documentation that Jack Lowe moved with the family for he seems to disappear from the family narrative. Again, we simply do not know all the facts, but we do know that it was a good move for Janie and her daughters for it allowed them to prosper.

Chapter 3: Montgomery

*Birdseye view of Dexter Avenue in Montgomery showing
early streetcar lines from an early postcard*

Jim Crow in the South

When the Cole-Lowe family moved from Clayton to
Montgomery, the city was, and still is, the capital city of
Alabama. Like most capital cities, it had a thriving
economic and social climate.

In 1886, the progressive city of Montgomery became
the first city in the U.S. to install city-wide electric
streetcars. The widespread routes enabled residents from
outside the city center to reach the center of town, the seat
of Alabama government, more efficiently. This modern
transportation system would soon allow Janie, who
through her sewing ability had become a Montgomery
businesswoman, to reach her high society clients making
her business life easier. Even on this modern

convenience, however, she was, as mandated by strict segregation laws, forced to sit in designated areas.

During her childhood, whether in Clayton or later in Montgomery, Annie lived in the Jim Crow confines of the post-Civil War South. Everything was segregated. "Whites only" and 'Colored" signs dotted her landscape. Most stores, churches, theaters, entrances to buildings, and of course, schools were so designated.

As Annie and Sallie rode public transportation during their youth, the buses and streetcars pictured here and on the following page, with their prominent color-based distinctions clearly marked, would have been the type they encountered.

Photo courtesy Encyclopedia of Alabama
Organization

*Photo courtesy Encyclopedia of Alabama
Organization.*

The following signs would have been seen in all public places as Annie and Sallie and other members of their race grew and played in Clayton and later Montgomery.

Photos courtesy Encyclopedia of Alabama Organization

Education

Annie's formal education, like that of her mother and sister before her, would have been received in the Black schools of early 20th Century segregated Alabama. While Ann's enrollment in the Alabama public school system cannot be verified, she later told an interviewer that she was in school until the age of fourteen.

For Black students, the school years were shorter, eighty-five days compared to one hundred twenty-seven days for white students, and attendance was not mandatory. Teachers in the Black schools were often undereducated and woefully underpaid. The settings found in most of these schools, no matter how hard the teachers tried, were inferior to those of nearby whites-only schools. Nevertheless, for the few years that she attended school, this was the setting in which she learned. With the support she found at home, Ann took what she could from these situations.

At home, her mother, grandmother, aunts, and even her big sister, were giving her equally important life lessons and skills. As they grew, both Sallie and Annie followed in the footsteps of the three female generations that preceded them and became skilled seamstresses. Annie, Sallie, Janie, and Georgia learned from each other and supported each other. Sallie and Annie remained close throughout their lives and in later years Annie would rely on Sallie for emotional and physical support.

With Janie leading the way, Georgia, and Jane became known for their expertly designed and stitched clothing. Drawing upon their talent, they were able to establish a successful business, designing and making lovely clothing, mostly evening, presentation, and debutante gowns, for Montgomery's women of society, eventually including the governor's wife and daughters. Even as fashions were changing, many of their patrons still requested the sweeping gowns from the earlier years. The Cole-Lowe women could easily provide such fashions.

During this time, young Annie, a keen observer, saw the variety and beauty of the flowers of her world. Her earliest introduction to flowers would have been in Clayton where native azaleas, dogwoods, and jasmine bushes grew wild. Living in Montgomery gave her the opportunity to see more manicured lawns, filled with camellias, roses, lilies, and magnolias along with the azaleas and dogwoods. Colorful annuals and perennials, carefully tended, lined the many sidewalks of the town.

At the same time, she was observing the equally impressive artistry and the impressive array of rich materials used by her mother and grandmother. As a youngster, she played for hours each day with the enticing scraps of fabric she found on the floor of her mother and grandmother's sewing room. As they sewed and designed, Annie spent her time designing and making dresses for her paper dolls and teaching herself to made fabric flowers. Her tiny hands used some of the most expensive fabrics available while perfecting her ability to make magical flowers.

Soon she was combining her love of flowers and her love of fabrics in her own artistic manner. Family history says that she designed her first dress at the age of five and was competently designing and making her own patterns by the age of ten

The happy hours she spent designing and making these earliest flowers led to a signature of her later clothing designs. Exquisite, handmade flowers, with no two alike, were to be found on almost every gown she later designed.

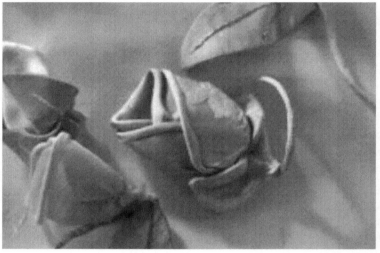

Another important skill and future design influence was passed to Annie during these young learning years. Mother, grandmother, and even great-grandmother, lived in a time when the use of quilting for clothing was quite common. Quilted petticoats were often used in the big plantation homes for an additional layer of warmth and to add fullness to the large gowns so favored by the southern ladies of the period. Almost assuredly her un-named great-grandmother who was the seamstress to the mistress of the plantation home passed on this technique to Georgia and through her, the tradition continued. The most decorative of these quilting techniques was trapunto. Trapunto quilting is a technique used to add another dimension to any fabric. Although used most often for quilts, it was also found on lingerie, outerwear, and tailored clothing. Hand trapunto, which the Cole-Lowe ladies would certainly have used, is tedious and time-consuming, but the result of this stuffing technique creates an elegant, sophisticated look. It was surely from her grandmother and her mother during these formative years that Ann learned the trapunto method of quilting. Soon she had perfected this difficult technique and later used it on many of her treasured garments.

Today's society often assumes that the Black women in the late 1800s and early 1900s wore out-of-style, hand-me-down, and worn out clothing made from whatever fabric (flour sack, feed sack, etc.) and scraps of fabric were on hand. While, of course, this is true of many women, both Black and white, who were struggling during those years, women of color wore fashionable styles as much as their white neighbors. The Cole-Lowe women would have been no exception for not only were Georgia, Janie, and other members of the family making beautiful clothing for their clients but also for themselves and other family members.

Throughout her formative years Annie, watched and learned as she grew in Clayton and Montgomery surrounded by creative women and beautiful fabrics while wearing stylish clothing herself. All the while, she was learning to design and create fashions that would one day enchant America's highest realm of society, winning her accolades from the ladies of that society as they delighted in her skills and designs.

The Cole-Lowe Women and the First Family of Alabama

Living in Montgomery provided a steady business atmosphere for the Cole-Lowe women. Jane became a dressmaker for the wife of the 34th governor of Alabama, Emmet O'Neal. Governor O'Neal was himself the son of a former governor of Alabama. Thus, he had grown up in society and always dressed to impress that society. He expected his wife Lizzie Kirkland O'Neal and their daughters to dress equally as well. Mrs. O'Neal, who, according to the local newspaper, the Montgomery Advisor, was well known for her grace and charm, was well-suited for the role of Alabama's First Lady.

Grace and charm, however, were not enough. Added pressure to 'look the part' was brought upon the ladies of Governor O'Neal's family in 1911 when they became the first family to occupy the official Governor's Mansion on South Perry Street in Montgomery. They finally had a fine, permanent home in which to showcase themselves and their social skills, and their wardrobe had to reflect their status. Jane, with the help of her mother Georgia and her young daughter Ann who had left school to become a part of the family business, provided designs and clothing that met the high expectations of the governor and his family The Cole-Lowe ladies, with their reliance on fine fabrics, sparkles, gold-colored embroidery, and voluminous skirts gave the O'Neal ladies what they needed to meet the expectations of Alabama society for several rewarding years.

In 1914 Jane was working to complete an order for four gowns for Mrs. Kirkland O'Neal when she suddenly became ill and died shortly thereafter. Nothing more is known about her illness and death, just that it was sudden.

Sixteen year old Ann, although grieving, knew the importance of the order her mother was working on and with a hint of the determination that she would demonstrate later in her career, stepped into her mother's place, completed the commission, and, to everyone's pleasure, delivered the beautiful gowns to Mrs. O'Neal on time. This accomplishment gave Ann the feeling that "there was nothing I couldn't do when it came to sewing." Her career had begun.

After her mother's death, even though she was married by this time, Ann, along with her grandmother Georgia and other family members, continued the family business of dressing the society women of Montgomery. At the same time, Annie was developing a fashion flair all her own and when she was out and about, one saw a very stylish young Black woman.

Janey's gravestone, found in the Pioneer Black Cemetery in Clayton seems enlightened by time for it was obviously written and erected in her memory many years after her death. It reads as follows:

"Jane Cole Lowe
186?-1914
Mother of Anne Lowe, Fashion designer."

Even as her fame in Alabama grew, Ann along with all others of her race, still felt the sting of segregation. She still saw and was expected to obey the "white's only" signs that distinguished white facilities from 'colored' facilities in her world.

Perhaps this obvious discrimination was one reason why, as she gained control of her life and career, most of her clients were from the white upper class of society. Through those clients she not only had access to places that would otherwise have been off limits to her, but she also could control some of the circumstances of her life. She was welcomed into her clients' homes as a valued employee, even if there were times when she was still told to use the back door!

GOVERNOR'S MANSION, MONTGOMERY, ALA.

Photo courtesy of Alabama Archives.

Built in 1906, this Beaux Arts brownstone served as the home of Alabama governors 1911-1950. In 1963 it was demolished to make way for the interstate highway. Both Jane and Ann would have been received there with their products. The house was located on the southwest corner of South Perry and South Streets, Montgomery, AL.

Perry Avenue, home of many of Alabama's socialites, 1916.
Photo courtesy of Library of Congress

FLORIDA

Introduction

"I left my husband today. I packed my belongings, grabbed my young son, and sought my freedom. My Great-Grandmother was enslaved, her every move controlled by others. My grandmother, for a good part of her life, was enslaved. I will not be. It is 1916. I will not be enslaved.

Last week while in a major Alabama department store, I felt someone's eyes following me. This is not unusual, for we Negros are always watched when in public, but I often visit this smaller store for I know the owners, and have never felt threatened there.

Still, on that day, I knew I was being watched. Slowly I looked around looking for an unhappy white customer or some low-life man who might be eyeing me. There was just me, an elderly woman leaning on her cane as she talked with a sales clerk while examining a display of dismal looking suits, and a smartly dressed white woman across the store looking at the finer dresses stocked by the owners. I went back to my browsing. I could hear the sales clerk and the elderly woman still deep in conversation. Soon the feeling of being watched returned. Could it be the well-dressed woman? Why? She had not looked disapproving of me, so why would she be watching me?

I concocted a plan. I would catch her at it. I turned as far away from her as possible, settled my face into a sweet smile, and abruptly turned trying to catch her off guard.

Instead, she caught me off guard, for there she was just four feet from me with a genuinely sweet smile on her face. I must have looked startled for she quickly apologized and introduced herself. 'Mrs. Josephine Lee, from Tampa, Florida,' she said. She wanted to know where I purchased my dress and hat.

My world changed immediately."

Chapter 4: Tampa

Tampa, Florida: "Franklin Street, looking North". Scanned from postcard, c. 1920 (?). "Pub. by S. H. Kress & Co." no date, no notice of any copyright. (S.H. Kress & Co. is the commercial "ancestor" of K-Mart.)

The Lee Family

Mrs. Josephine Lee from Tampa, Florida, was the wife of a wealthy Floridian. She and her husband, a successful Tampa businessman, had a family of two sons and four daughters, ages twelve to twenty-one. Her husband was a member of a leading family in the citrus industry and provided well for his family allowing Mrs. Lee and her daughters to be members of Tampa's elite social set. Impressive gowns and day dresses were always needed.

In addition, there was a wedding in the family's future, but not an ordinary wedding, a double wedding with the family's twin sisters as the brides. 'Could Ann, would Ann', Mrs. Lee asked her on the day they met, come to Tampa and design and make dresses for her daughters' trousseaux.

Ann was thrilled by the possibility but quickly realized there was a problem; she was married and had a son, Arthur. In 1912 Ann had married Andrew Lee Cohen (later changed to Cone). Years later Ann described her husband as 'a colored man who owned a chain of dress shops' and 'as old as my mother.' Their son Arthur was born a month before Ann's sixteenth birthday.

After her mother's death, as Ann became more heavily involved in her family's business, her husband became increasingly unhappy about it. He soon demanded that Ann give up her involvement in the business. He wanted, he said, a stay-at-home wife and mother. Reluctantly, Ann complied with her husband's wishes. She limited her dreams and designs to designing for herself and her family.

She was, however, never happy with her husband's demands and her submission to them; thus, when Mrs. Lee made her offer, Ann made the daring decision to leave her husband, take her young son, and follow Mrs. Lee to Tampa. Resolutely, Ann and young Arthur soon boarded a southbound train for Tampa, and Mr. Cohen soon divorced her. For the second time in a few years, Ann's career was about to take a giant leap forward.

In an interview, Ann later explained. *"It was, a chance to make all the lovely gowns I'd always dreamed about."*

The Lee family lived just north of Tampa in the Lake Thonotosassa area. They enjoyed an elegant home complete with servant quarters where Ann and her son lived for a while after their 1916 arrival.

The family soon loved Annie and her designs and immediately put her to work doing what she loved. She was once again working with sophisticated fabrics, brocades, lace, silk, and taffeta, designing and making numerous stylish gowns for the women in the family.

The two eldest daughters were twins and preferred to dress alike, even as adults. While this might have been challenging for Ann who prided herself in never making the same dress twice, she quickly became adept at dressing the girls and provided them the wedding dresses of their dreams.

The local paper, The *Tampa Daily Times* states, "The brides wore beautiful wedding gowns of white satin, embroidered in silver and pearls, and trimmed with exquisite lace. The gowns were both fashioned with long trains, and the brides wore tulle veils caught up with orange blossom wreaths."

There was no mention in the article of the gowns being exact replicas of each other. Ann, with her talent and her fierce desire to never design the same gown twice, would probably have interjected just enough design detail to make the gowns 'almost' identical but with just enough difference to give each bride her own special Annie Cole dress. We'll never know for the gowns no longer exist.

Ann also designed the brides' matching trousseaux and provided gowns for the bridesmaids, ribbon bearers, and flower girls. The brides' youngest sister Nell was one of the ribbon bearers at the ceremony. As described by the Tampa Daily Times, she wore a dress of "gold cloth and tulle trimmed with lace and carried a streamer with a ribbon of matching cloth down the aisle." The brides' seventeen-year-old sister Grace was one of the bridesmaids. The *Tampa Daily Times* described her gown simply as a 'very becoming creation of golden fabric with which she wore a golden picture hat."

After the wedding, Ann remained with the family as their seamstress and designer. She had a full load for she was sewing, not only for the sisters but also for Mrs. Lee who was always in demand and enjoyed looking her very best when going out. As the well-known and well-liked Lee ladies wore Ann's one-of-a-kind designs with pride, their friends were soon begging for an *"Annie Cole"* as her early labels identified her work. With the Lee's support, Ann complied with the many requests and her first independent business venture was born.

The Lee family recognized Ann's talents but knew that she needed some formal design education. In 1917 when Ann expressed interest in attending the S. T. Taylor School of Design in New York City, they encouraged her to do so. With their blessing, and perhaps financial backing, Ann left her comfortable place as Tampa's design darling and began her classes at S.T. Taylor.

Upon her arrival, Ann was to find that even there in New York, away from the Jim Crow South, she would face discrimination. The director of the school had only become acquainted with Ann through correspondence. No photo nor word of her race was asked for or given. Upon seeing her for the first time, he appeared not to be expecting anyone of color.

As Ann remembered it years later, the director did

not think she had the money necessary to attend. She showed him her bankbook and he allowed her to stay, but she perceived that he wanted to send her away. Although he did not, the other students refused to work and study with a Negro. Thus, she was segregated and worked and studied alone in a separate classroom. Most students and teachers at the school did not think a Negro girl from the South would succeed in the fashion design world. Ann persevered, however, for she was now assuredly pursuing her dream. She later remembered that her designs were soon leaving her solitary classroom and being used as examples for the other students. She completed her two-year program in one year and soon afterward she and Arthur returned to Tampa and to her friends, the Lees.

The Florida to which Ann returned in the early 1920s was a very busy place. Florida, more than any other state, experienced one of the greatest economic and social revolutions in American history. The state was changed forever as hundreds of thousands of Americans, poor, rich, good, bad, white, Black, and immigrants all came to Florida during this roaring decade.

Why did they come? The Florida Land Boom. Americans and others could afford to come to this land of sunshine and promises and come they did. The railroads made it possible for travelers to venture further into the state than ever before. Both chugging trains and recently produced automobiles brought new settlers. Tampa, with its nearby beaches, sunshine, and waterways, did not escape the migration, but in fact, became a much sought after location. Money poured into Tampa as wealthy northerners moved in and joined the wealthy Tampa social class. These families quickly adopted the social traditions of the day and supported all things exciting in the city, including Tampa's yearly celebration of Gasparilla.

It was in this atmosphere that Annie celebrated her birthday. She had reason to celebrate. This young woman from Alabama was the design darling of Tampa. She now owned her own dress/design shop in the fast-growing market of southwest Florida and employed eighteen dressmakers who completed her designs to her high expectations. She had also recently married for the second time. Marriage records from Hillsborough County, Florida, show that Ann and Caleb West, a hotel bellman, were married October 6, 1919. The U.S. Census records of 1920 show that she and Mr. Caleb West, husband and wife, were living in Tampa, Ward 5. Arthur Lee Cohen, Ann's son age 5, was living with them. This second marriage, like the first, did not last, but it did last longer. Before he left, however, according to the 1930 U.S. Census, they would have over 10 years together and later he would make a major move away from Tampa with Ann and her son. Later in life, Ann often explained why her second marriage failed.

"My husband left me. He said he wanted a real wife, not one who was forever jumping out of bed to sketch dresses."

Afternoon Tea Dress 1920s

Photo courtesy of the Lee family.

The Afternoon Tea Dress

Sometime during the 1920s, Ann designed and produced what in some circles was called an "Afternoon Tea Dress," and in other circles, a "Lingerie Dress." It was made of lightweight organdy and lace in black and white. The style had been popular in the late 1800s and early 1900s when ladies often socialized with 'afternoon teas.' In the 1920s, someone in the Lee family needed a new afternoon dress for social functions and turned to Ann. Between the wishes of the wearer and Ann, a dress was designed

The dress features puffed mid-length sleeves, perfect for Tampa afternoons, and a full skirt. The sleeves and the skirt have black lace inserts in a zigzag pattern. It is very sheer and requires an underskirt which Ann designed but which has been lost.

The dress is important to the Lee family as a beloved heirloom passed from generation to generation it is still occasionally worn. The small imperfections caused by wear and time do not detract from the family's love for the dress.

The dress holds an important place in Ann's story because it is one of the earliest extant examples of her work.

Gasparilla

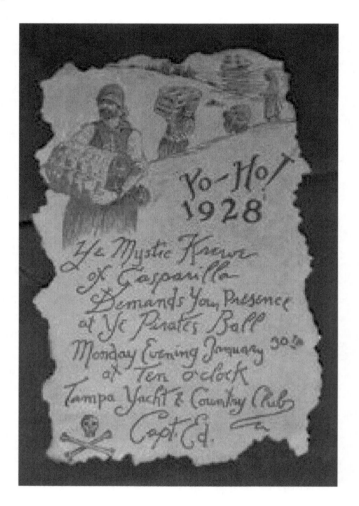

At the time of Ann's return to Tampa from New York City, Gasparilla had been a Tampa tradition for fifteen years. What began as the city's first May festival in 1904 had become one of the social highlights of the year, not only for the reigning social class but also for all area residents and visitors alike. Named for Jose Gaspar, a pirate who supposedly died and left untold fortune buried in and around Tampa, parades, music, and balls became the trademark of the weeklong celebration. It is, still today, Tampa's answer to Mardi Gras with a court and queen crowned each year.

Upon her return, Ann found the Lee women and their friends heavily involved with Gasparilla. This was Ann's time to shine, to show what she had learned at the hands and feet of her mother and grandmother and refined in her year of study. This was her chance to use and produce hundreds of handmade flowers as design features for ball gowns, presentation gowns, and of course, for the Queen and attendants of the Gasparilla Court. Costumes, based upon Pirate themes were also in vogue. It was Ann's time to stretch her imagination and design outside her comfort zone. It was the beginning of good things for Annie Cole Lowe.

Designing for Gasparilla

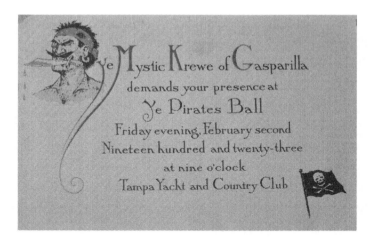

Ye Mystic Krewe of Gasparilla
demands your presence at
Ye Pirates Ball
Friday evening, February second
Nineteen hundred and twenty-three
at nine o'clock
Tampa Yacht and Country Club

A coveted invitation to the 1923 Gasparilla Pirates Ball surely called for an Ann Cole original gown. This invitation was for the special event at the Tampa Yacht and Country Club in celebration of Gasparilla.

Although she excelled at designing and producing all types of clothing, it was the ball gowns and cotillion or presentation gowns with their full, flowing skirts, that still seemed to most touch Ann's heart. As Gasparilla approached each year, the wealthy patrons and debutantes of society approached Ann with the hope that she would be able to clothe them for the many events to come. Some of Ann's Gasparilla gowns were of her familiar elegant billowing design, but she had learned that Gasparilla was a different type of venue than that of the social activities of Montgomery.

For a few years in the 1920s the Gasparilla organizers select a yearly theme for the event. In the early 1920s, after the discovery of the tomb of Tutankhamun,

Egyptian fever seized the country. In 1924 Ann began a multi-year agreement with an organization named "Ye Mystic Krewe of Gasparilla." In that year the theme was Egypt and all things Gasparilla that year reflected that theme, including Ann's festival designs through which she was able to let her imagination, talent, and fashion sense take her into new and exciting, creative avenues.

Thus, she designed and sewed for the court creating elaborate costumes in the Egyptian motif. While the courts' costumes are lost to time, a description of the Gasparilla queen's gown for that year remains. Queen Sarah Keller's Ann Lowe gown was described as fashioned of white Mollo O'Crepe satin adorned with silver and rhinestone embroidered in shafts of wheat. It was a slim fit with a triple train attached to the gown with wings of rhinestones. The rounded neck was beaded. Ms. Keller later said it reminded her of Cleopatra's robes.

As the years passed, the organization left the theme approach leaving Ann and the ladies of the court free to allow their design desires full reign. Unfortunately few of the Gasparilla gowns still exist, but the memories of those days and those gowns live on in the families of those young women who wore an Ann Lowe gown. In 1965 a *Tampa Tribune* article paid tribute to Ann. Women who had worn her creations forty years earlier were still raving about their incredible designer. These ladies could recall their Annie Cole dresses in detail.

One socialite talked about Ann and her Gasparilla gowns. *"If you didn't have a Gasparilla gown by Annie, you may as well stay home."*

Gasparilla Queen of 1924, Sarah Keller Hobbs sentimentally recalled *"there was not anyone like Annie."*

A story is told that Ann once remarked that she had designed many gowns for Gasparilla and other Tampa affairs, but had never been to an event that called for her gowns. In other words, she had never seen them in the setting for which they were designed. Nell Keene, Gasparilla Queen in 1926, knew Ann through the Lee family. After Ann's remark about her exclusion, Nell invited her to attend a ball. Some say it was a Gasparilla Ball and some say it was a different ball. At any rate, Ann accepted.

The story continues, that many in attendance did not approve of Ann's inclusion. It seems that in the eyes of the attendees, her race trumped her prestige in designing the exquisite dresses for the ceremony.

This incident, however, did not dampen Ann's memories or love for Tampa. She always recalled her Tampa years with great fondness and later called them *"the happiest years of my life,"*

In 1976 Ann sent a message to the ladies of Tampa who might still remember her. *"Tell them I love each and every one. In my mind they are young, beautiful, and excited about a wedding, Gasparilla, or a party...those memories bring me great happiness."*

Chapter 5: Gasparilla Gowns
Portfolio I

The Evening Shift

The evening shift on the following page, believed to be one of the earliest examples of Ann's designs, shows her emerging diversity in Tampa. Following the dictates not only of the Gasparilla governing body, but also of the time period itself, the shift demonstrates a distinct difference from the gowns Ann grew up watching her mother and grandmother design and make.

Fashioned about 1924, it was worn for an evening event by Gasparilla Queen, Ms. Sarah Keller. This clearly shows not only Ann's talent but also her desire to give her clients what they wanted. The dress is an example of the Roaring Twenties with a nod to the theme that year, Egypt. It is a hand-sewn sleeveless dress made of yellow and gold silk faille fabric with intricate floral designs. Featured are large pink and green beaded flowers and a two inch wide band of rows with silver rocaille, a French-inspired decoration that relied heavily on cascades of flowers, leaves, palm trees, and other natural elements. This dress is historically significant as the earliest confirmed example of Ann's work.

The Evening Shift

Photo courtesy of Henry Plant Museum Society
Gasparilla Collection, Tampa, Florida

1920's Red

The following dress, from 1926 is another design that was very different from her usual style and again shows how Ann could adapt to her clients' needs. The dress colorfully captures the society of the 1920s before the Stock Market Crash. It is short, flirty, and dazzling with rhinestones. It was worn by Ms. Katherine Broaddus (Livingston), a maid in the 1926 Gasparilla Court. It is made of Metallic gauze over red silk fabric lining featuring an ornate starburst design made of hand-sewn rhinestones, red sequin beads, and red jeweled stones. The upper left shoulder has a large jeweled medallion. The right shoulder supports a red jeweled spaghetti strap. There are smaller medallions near the hem of the dress.

1920s Red

Photo courtesy of Henry Plant Museum Society,
Gasparilla Collection, Tampa, Florida

Gasparilla Court 1928

Shown below is the gown Ann created for the 1928 Queen Emala Parkhill. This gown gave Ann a chance to again design a large skirt billowing with flowers. Pictured is Queen Emala and her Royal Court of Gasparilla, 1928

Photo from: http://ymkg.com/kings-queens-1921-1929/

Gasparilla Court 1929

Here you can see the entire Gasparilla Royal Court in their Ann Lowe designs.

Gasparilla 1957

The gown on the following page is evidence that even though Ann was no longer living in Tampa, she was still designing for Gasparilla as late as 1957. The change in fashion design can be seen, but the attention to craftsmanship was still as strong as ever. Below is the Gasparilla Jewel Circle gown worn by Ms. Rebecca Davies Smith in 1957.

This more modern gown is made of cream- colored satin with a sweetheart bodice made to be worn just off the shoulders. There are concealed spaghetti straps for Ms. Davies' comfort and an inner boned corset. The bodice is adorned with strands of beads and small pearls which form delicate twisting vine forms and Ann's ever present flowers. Layers of sheer light blue tulle netting line the top of the bodice, the sleeves, and the short train which is attached to the gown at the back of the waist.

Photo courtesy of Henry Plant Museum Society, Gasparilla Collection, Tampa, Florida

PART II: NEW YORK AND BEYOND

NEW YORK AND PARIS

Introduction

"*Looking back, I remember the day as if it were yesterday. I carefully folded my newest creation, wrapped it in tissue paper, and placed it on top of my other designs in the trunk that would sail with me to Paris, I smiled to myself imagining the trip I was about to take.*

"*A trip to Paris. During Fashion Week!*

"*It was 1949 and only ten years ago such a trip would have seemed incomprehensible, yet here I was about to embark upon this trip of a lifetime. Although I was going to the fashion capital of the world, I was not going as the designer I truly was, but as a fashion journalist, but I was happy, for that was close enough. At least for the moment.*

"*I had no designs in the show, my fashion magic was just beginning its climb up the American social ladder. Nevertheless, my talent and knowledge had caught the eyes of the editors of the New York Age, a major African American newspaper, and they were sending me to cover this first major Paris Fashion Week since the end of WWII.*

"*Still, I knew my designs would be there. I would see to that for I would showcase my designs on my own body. I designed all my own clothing, and created my personal pieces with the same care I extended to my clients, so I knew I would be wearing a dignified, well-fitting wardrobe worthy of a first class designer.*

"*I did not expect to be recognized as the designer I was, for I knew I would be seated with the other journalists, slightly apart from the designers, models, lovely fabrics, and true excitement. I also knew I might even be looked upon as an outsider, me with my chocolate skin and my tiny body. Still, I was going. I would observe, learn, report, and rejoice in the moment.*

"At the same time, a young Parisian designer was about to show his designs under his own label for the first time at a major fashion show. He was about to change the world of fashion forever.

"Thus, with my reporter's notebook and pen in hand, I packed my bags and anticipated the upcoming week with excitement.

"So, too, did Christian Dior."

Who was this middle-aged woman so carefully packing her creations and her dreams as she looked ahead to a crossing the Atlantic? She was the current member in a long line of family seamstress designers.

When she finally sat to contemplate her coming trip, her thoughts tripped over themselves as she tried to imagine the reactions from her mother Janey and her grandmother Georgia if they could somehow know of little Annie's good fortune.

"From your slavery to my freedom to do this, Grandmama, I wish you could know."

Chapter 6: New York

New York, 1930

A 1930s view of part of Manhattan.
Photo from the public domain.

Harlem

It was 1928, the Stock Market had not yet crashed, and the Harlem Renaissance was in full swing when Ann arrived in New York City. Some sources state that her second husband, Caleb West did not make the move with her. Yet, the 1930 U.S. Census for New York tells a different story. According to that Census, Ann, husband Caleb, son Arthur, Alabama cousin Tommie Mae Cole, and two boarders had settled together in the Central Harlem area. This was an appropriate area for Ann for in the 1920s and 30s Central and West Harlem were the focus of the Harlem Renaissance. There Ann and her little family joined the thousands of artistic, educated Black Americans who migrated to this capital of Black America.

The uniqueness of this renaissance was the outpouring of artistic work by the Black community as Harlem's cultural awareness led to the expansion of ideas and creativity among the Negro community. Many of Harlem's people left a lasting impression on American culture: Duke Ellington, Langston Hughes, Billie Holiday, Louis Armstrong, Zora Neale Hurston, Myles Davis, and Ralph Ellison, just to name a few.

Fashion was an important part of the movement. Ann's artistic talent made this area a natural choice for her and her family and the name Ann Cole Lowe, though unknown to most at the time, should be added to that list of Harlem Renaissance achievers.

Harlem became the home of the Black Fashion Museum. Opened by Lois K. Alexander-Lane in 1979 in a Harlem brownstone, the museum showcased fashion items from the African American fashion community. At one point there were over 2000 items in the museum's collection. Many of those items were accessories, but some dresses and gowns were housed there including some of Ann Lowe's work. In 2007 the Black Fashion Museum collection was donated to the Smithsonian National Museum of African American History and Culture by Mrs. Alexander-Lane's daughter, Joyce Bailey.

Harlem brownstone street scenes in the 1920s and 30s.
Photo from the public domain.

The Apollo: One of Harlem's favorites.
Photo from the Public Domain

In 1929 CBS began broadcasting from
Harlem's Cotton Club   *Photo from the public domain.*

The City

Ann joined the New York City scene shortly before the Stock Market crashed and America was thrown into the Great Depression. Soon economic fear spread and millions of Americans were standing in soup lines. Consumer spending and investment dropped dramatically affecting all walks of life. Unemployment was rampant and by 1933 thirteen to fifteen million Americans were unemployed and banks were failing daily. New York City was not exempt from the misery caused by this depression.

As the economic world around her disappeared, Ann could have turned and headed back to the safety of Tampa where she knew work awaited her. She didn't turn, and she didn't run for she still held fast to her dream.

To accomplish what she wanted she established a small shop in a third floor loft and began making a name for herself in the competitive fashion design market. Still money was tight, so to ensure that money would be coming into the household, she also began working for other design houses, houses with a reach beyond the poverty of the masses and into the loftier realms of society. While working for these houses, they attached their design labels, not hers, to her designs. They kept the lions' share of the profits. Still, she knew that to become the success she wanted to be, she must persevere and make a name for herself. Eventually the labels, while still carrying the name of the firm she was working for, did also carry Ann's name.

Through the 1930s and 1940s, as Ann struggled and dreamed, she never gave up. She was on a steady path, working hard to fulfill those dreams. She never wavered in her belief that New York City was the place in which she would achieve them.

Ann's label while designing for the A.F. Chantilly Company of New York.
Photo courtesy of Metropolitan Museum of Art
www.metmuseum.org

Being in New York City gave Ann a front-row seat from which to view many important historical events of the day. This young woman from rural Alabama and the flatlands of Florida was in the right spot to see skyscrapers reach higher and higher into the sky above her. In 1931, the Empire State Building surpassed the one-year-old Chrysler Building as the tallest in the world and the entire city celebrated. She was still a New Yorker forty years later when the World Trade Center finally surpassed the Empire State Building in height.

Empire State Building, 1940s. Photo courtesy of Getty Images.

In 1935 history hit closer to home for Ann when the arrest of a shoplifter inflamed racial tensions in Harlem and soon escalated to rioting and looting.

She might have gazed with wonder in 1936 when the Hindenburg flew over New York City, passing Manhattan.

Photo from the public domain.

She was nearby for the opening of the Lincoln Tunnel, for the 1939 New York World's Fair, for the founding of the American Negro Theatre, and when New York's first two TV stations went on the air.

She watched as New York held its first Fashion Week in 1943. It was, in fact, the first fashion week ever held, ahead of the Paris and London markets. Ann was not invited to participate, but she did watch with interest.

She again saw the Empire State Building make headlines when in 1945 a B-25 Bomber accidently crashed into the 79th floor killing 13 people. Back home in Alabama and Tampa, folks could only read about these events. Ann could witness them.

The 1930s came to a close, and the likelihood of war was realized as World War II engulfed the world,

Americans began to see a promising upswing in their prosperity for war manufacturing was helping the American economy. The fashion industry was not one of the fastest industries to recover, and Ann was still working for others while struggling to make a name for herself.

By the 1940 U.S. Census, Ann was listed as head of household. She was identified as a widow even though years later she said her second husband left her. In this census, there were only two in the household---Ann and Sallie. Sometime between 1935 and 1940, her sister Sallie had joined her in her Harlem apartment, but Caleb, Arthur, Tommie Mae, and all her boarders are gone. It was the beginning of life as they would know it for years to come. Records indicate that Sallie and Ann shared their Harlem apartment for over 30 years.

During these war years and afterward, Ann and Sallie would have seen and heard the many activities that took place in New York City that related to the war. Bond Drives and parades were common. Included in these parades would have been the January 1946 New York City ticker-tape Victory Parade led by the 13,000 men of the 82nd Airborne Division, including the African-American Parachute Infantry Battalion.

Later, the two would have watched history, not from their sidewalk but from a world away. Although away from the turmoil of the South, Ann must have watched in wonder at the changes being brought about in her ancestral homeland. One can only imagine her astonishment when another petite seamstress from Alabama refused to give up her seat on the bus, one of those seats traditionally reserved for white passengers, and started a boycott that led to a movement that resulted in changes Ann might never have imagined. This time, however, Ann was not watching the history up close, but from afar.

An Unusual Wedding Dress

Photo courtesy of Metropolitan Museum of Art.
Gift of Mrs. K. Fenton Trimingham, Jr., 1975 Accession number:
1975: 349a,b: www.metmuseum.org

In the early 1940's one of Ann's clients provided her with an important stepping stone. Ann was commissioned to design a unique wedding dress for this client. It was 1941, and she was designing for A.F. Chantilly.

Although Ann preferred the big billowing dresses, she always listened to her clients and gave them what they wanted, not what she wanted. This dress exemplifies her desire to please her client. There was no billowing skirt, no tulle, and no hand-made flowers. Instead, it was long and slim and made of shinning synthetic fabric.

From the *New York Times* we have this description. "The bride wore a gown of white satin, the skirt ending in an oval twenty-foot train. The neckline was embellished with white satin Bermuda lilies embroidered with seed pearls, continuing down the center panel in a design of stems."

The gown exemplified Ann's insistence on perfection. When examined, inside and out, the detailing and finishing on the gown are perfection and the work is considered a treasure.

Although not on display, the dress is now owned by the Metropolitan Museum of Art. It has been said that this dress and the client for whom it was created were financially important to Ann and her early career in New York.

The Oscars

Award-winning Actress Olivia de Havilland modeling her Ann Lowe
gown.
Photo courtesy Oscars.org 1947

Even though Ann was not personally interested in designing for movie stars some of the design houses she worked for certainly were interested. This interest linked Ann to the 19th Academy Awards, presented in 1947 for the best of the 1946 Hollywood year. 1946 was the first full year since the end of WWII and the awards that year continued the recent trend that Oscar voters had established of honoring films about contemporary social issues. The best picture award went to *The Best Years of Our Lives* which centered around the lives of three returning veterans as they tried to adjust to life after the war.

The award for best actress went to Olivia de Havilland in *To Each His Own* for her portrayal of an unwed mother who considers terminating her pregnancy but decides against it and gives birth to her son. It was a melodrama certain to bring tears to the audience.

When the time came for Miss de Havilland to choose a gown for Oscar night, she went to Sonia Rosenberg's salon. Ann was working for Sonia at the time and one of Ann's designs was selected. She not only designed but also made the flower studded gown worn by Olivia de Havilland as she accepted her Best Actress Oscar

Photo courtesy Oscars.org

This photo provides an up-close look at some of the hand-sewn and painted flowers adorning Olivia de Havilland's Ann Lowe gown. 1947.

Olivia de Havilland with Ray Milland after accepting her Oscar
while wearing her Ann Lowe gown. 1947.
Photos and quote courtesy Oscars.org.

Later when recalling that evening, Ms. De Haviland
recalled an incident at dinner before the Oscar
presentation.

*"When I was nominated for 'To Each His Own,' I
wore a pale blue organza dress that had a marvelous
hand-painted garland. Before going to the ceremony I
went to a dinner party. As our host was ladling Madeira*

sauce onto my baked ham, he sprinkled me liberally with sauce. Every napkin at the table was used to try to rub it out. Luckily, most fell on the garland so you really couldn't see it. But I accepted my first Oscar wearing Madeira Sauce undetected by even the sharpest eyes."

OLIVIA DE HAVILLAND
Unknown

Unknown? Not really!

Throughout all these years, Ann never faltered in her belief that she had made the right decision when she left Tampa. She believed in herself, her decision, and she worked daily, sketching and sewing, to achieve her dream. Forty years after moving to New York, Ann was asked by an *Oakland Tribune* reporter why she left Tampa.

"I just knew that if I could come to New York and make dresses for society people my dreams would be fulfilled."

Chapter 7: World Traveler

New York to Paris: Late '40s

Photo courtesy of Library of Congress: Public Domain

Lowe and Dior

WWII had been over for several years. The entire world was trying to right itself again and fashion houses of Paris were making plans. The beautiful world of fashion had not died during the horrifying years of WWII. That world, however, had been quite different during those years, even in Paris.

Paris, like the rest of France and much of Europe, had been occupied by enemy troops. The citizens lived under strict rules and regulations. Parisians had seen curfews, shortages, death and destruction. Under these conditions, fashion continued but with less flamboyance and fewer participants for at one point or another, an estimated two-thirds of Parisians, usually the very wealthy patrons of haute couture, fled Paris for the French countryside hoping the war would not follow them. It often did.

In New York during the war, the socialites did not need to flee to the countryside, but the depression of the 1930s and war-time shortages of the 1940s had certainly curtailed social life. In both countries, worry and concerns for the welfare of the men and women fighting to save the world cast a somber mood upon society and the fashion world.

Back in Paris after the liberation, fashion once again became important and French fashion houses began to reopen. There was no doubt that soon Paris would be the scene of a lively Fashion Week.

Thus the late 40s announcement that Paris would host a Fashion Press Week was welcome news to all.

Ann Lowe and Christian Dior excitedly arrived in Paris. He was to achieve great success with his "New Look." Ann was to report on it. She didn't know it yet, but she was witnessing the birth of a fashion icon. What she did know was that she was seeing designs that she loved, especially Dior's "New Look" with figure-shaping suits and billowing gowns. The look would soon shake the fashion world. For our purposes, Ann was the most important designer at that Fashion Week. In the eyes of the rest of the fashion world, it soon became Dior.

They were so very different, yet so alike. He was from a wealthy French family, although his family had fallen on hard times. She was from a poor area of a poor state in the Deep South of America. He attended college; she left school after one year of high school. He had a degree in art; she did not.

Still, there were similarities. She loved designing, so did he. She spent years designing under the name of others, so did he. She loved voluminous skirts and trains, so did he, and she adorned her designs with many flowers as he did.

So different, yet so alike. Ann Lowe and Christian Dior.

"We were emerging from the period of war, of uniforms, of women-soldiers built like boxers. I drew women-flowers, soft shoulders, fine waists like liana, and wide skirts like corolla."
Christian Dior

Ann would have loved this 1947 Dior design with its
Voluminous skirt and sweeping train.
Photo from the public domain

Dior's 1947 "New Look."
Photo courtesy of House of Dior.

As the 40s gave way to the 50s, America's ladies of society traveled the world, and so, too, did Ann's designs. They were seen from London's drawing rooms to the salons of Paris and beyond.

On a later trip to Paris, Ann and Christian Dior were finally introduced. Mrs. Marjorie Merriweather Post, a client of Ann's, found the opportunity to introduce the two designers. By that time, Dior's fashions were marketed under the label "The House of Dior." Mrs. Merriweather Post introduced the two giving status to Ann by saying to Dior, *"She is the head of the American House of Lowe."* At another ball in Paris, Christian Dior greeted Joan Dillon, daughter of Ambassador to Paris, with *"Who made this gown?"* Miss Dillon answered that the dress was made by Ann Lowe, Dior is said to have replied, *"Give her my love."*

Years later, on one of her trips to Paris to observe the work of her peers, Ann recalled having tea with Dior. Thus, these two who had so excitedly ventured to Paris soon after WWII were getting to know each other's designs.

As their careers continued, differences became apparent. Christian Dior achieved great financial success. Ann Lowe did not. Fashion journalists developed a love affair with Christian Dior. They largely ignored Ann Lowe for years. Dior is one of the most remembered designers of his time. Ann, one of the least. After his death, just 10 years after the Paris Fashion Week, Christian Dior's label lived on. After her death, Ann's died with her.

Chapter 8: Post WWII

The 1950s and '60s

After the end of WWII, Winston Churchill observed that "America at this moment stands at the summit of the world." Americans seemed to believe this of themselves and their country. They were proud to assert that they had the strongest military, the strongest economy, and the strongest government in the world.

As America entered the decade of the 1950s, it was a country of paradoxes. A society desiring peace, but soon plagued by unrest. A society portrayed today as a loving family, content at home, yet the number of families in the 1950s who were uprooting and moving their families away from the familiar to the unfamiliar was growing by leaps and bounds. Today we remember the 1950s as the era of the Yankees in New York, the suburbs throughout the country, and Elvis—everywhere. It was *Leave it to Beaver* and *Father Knows Best,* poodle skirts, and rock and roll.

Through it all, Ann had a front row seat, but what was she most interested in during those days? Not the poodle skirts and the teenage hangouts on the corner. She still had her eye on the prize and she was interested in those who could give it to her…members of high society with their fancy evenings out, lavish weddings, nights at the opera and, of course, debutante balls.

It has been said that Ann designed over 2,000 wedding gowns, ball gowns, and coming out or debutante dresses in the 1950s and early 1960s, always listening to her clients, but always creating her one-of-a-kind gowns. Additionally, tea gowns, evening gowns, and opera gowns continued to roll from her artistic mind to her nimble fingers. So, too, did her afternoon dresses and her fashions for herself and her family. She and Sallie, who worked alongside Ann for years, and their assistants continued to please and astound her clients. Debutantes, brides, and society's social stars knew they would look their best, and be the belle of the ball, in an Ann Lowe original.

As fashion changed, Ann changed with it, she could fashion less elaborate, simple, sophisticated gowns if that is what her clients requested. Still, there would be an element of Ann Lowe design to be found in each of them. They may have been less sophisticated, but they were never simple or boring. One such dress was a strapless pink satin gown with a sweeping 10 feet train, embroidered with red glitter. Other gowns were tightly fitted, but with sweeping coats or trains. Scattered on most would have been one-of-a-kind flowers, beads, stitching, and other embellishments.

Throughout these years, however, Ann's penchant for overlooking financial matters was taking its toll. Her interest was the design of the dress, the joy that it brought her. In the end, this proved to be disastrous.

Ann's working arrangement with other designers and stores had taken her through the depression years and World War II. During that time she worked for Henri Bendel, Neiman Marcus, Saks Fifth Avenue, and others, but by 1950 she had reached her goal of owning her own design studio in New York City for she was able to open a small dress salon on Madison Avenue. She changed her label from the Ann Cole and Annie Cohen labels of Tampa, to Ann Lowe, a name that soon became known to the wealthy New York, Philadelphia, Boston, and Washington women of society.

Photo Courtesy of Metropolitan Museum of Art.
www.metmuseum.org.

These clients knew her for her elegant gowns made from luxurious fabrics and adorned with delicate hand-made flowers. These flowers often took weeks of intricate work to make. The ladies knew that, except for bridesmaid dresses, no two Ann Lowe dresses were ever alike. They also knew that she would listen to their wishes and work her magic to integrate their desires with her impeccable designs thus giving them enchanting gowns.

Ann added beading, fringe, and delicate but ornamental details. Then, with hand-sewn seams featuring the tiniest of stitches, she gave the wearer a perfect fit, proportionate to her figure alone. On the all-important inside of the gown, she often added lightly boned bodices if she knew dancing would be involved for such a bodice structure held the bosom stable on the dance floor. Ann often added bras to her designs for the ease of her clients. She wanted the elegant matrons and debutantes of society to be able to "step in and go."

In these photos, one can see the inside of several of Ann's creations. You'll see small bra cups for support, bone for stiffening , elastic for support, waistline support, and lace seams for comfort, along with interior linings, labels and more.

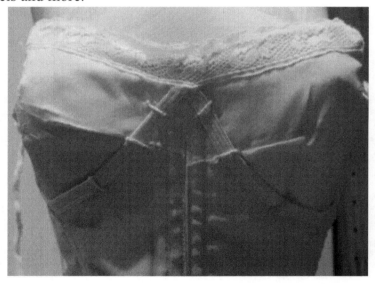

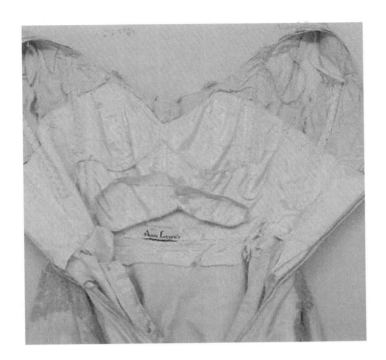

Soon Ann's salon, by her accounting, was making as many as 1,000 gowns a year. It was during this time that Ann became what she called a *"design snob."* She described what she meant by that.

"I love my clothes," she said, *"and I'm particular about who wears them. I am not interested in sewing for café society or social climbers. I do not cater to Mary and Sue. I sew for the families of the Social Register."*

Thus, her clientele were members of the top realm of society. Those ladies, like Ann, were design snobs and didn't want just anyone hiring Ann so they kept her identity a close-knit secret among themselves. Society women were said to have secretly passed her name around among themselves but not to outsiders. She was, called, *"Society's Best-Kept Secret,"* by Thomas Congdon in the December 1966 issue of *The Saturday Evening Post.*

Who were those ladies who relied on this elegantly dressed, soft-spoken woman from the South? Their names filled the social registers and society pages of the day: Rockefeller, Roosevelt, DuPont, Lodge, Post, Whitney, Dillon, Biddle, Rothschild, Smith, Jarett, Auchincloss, and Bouvier among others.

These were the ladies for whom Ann chose to design and sew. As she said, she chose them as much as they chose her, and they were glad she did. A few years later, Ann's name briefly joined theirs in the Society Register.

The matrons and young married women of this group were enjoying the postwar years with evenings at the opera, galas, and elegant balls. The younger members of these socially elite families were just the right age to wear debutante dresses fashioned by Ann Lowe.

ANN LOWE: SOCIETY'S BEST-KEPT SECRET

By Thomas H. Congdon Jr.

From the Saturday Evening Post article by Thomas Cogdon, Jr.

"A dress is a piece of ephemeral architecture, designed to enhance the proportions of the female body."

Christian Dior

Ms. Marjorie Merriweather Post 1952

Formal portrait of Mrs. Marjorie Merriweather Post
1952, by Douglas Chandor. Ph*oto courtesy of Hillwood
Estate, Museum and Gardens, Archives and
Special Collections*

One of the loveliest and most influential of the matrons for whom Ann designed was Ms. Marjorie Merriweather Post, heiress to the Post Cereal Company (later General Mills). Mrs. Merriweather Post was a well-known and well-liked businesswoman and fashion leader who valued beauty, elegance, and grace. In 1952 when posing for a formal portrait by painter Douglas Candor, she chose to wear an Ann Lowe gown. The gown is described as silver waffle weave silk faille.

Mr. Candor began Mrs. Merriweather Post's portrait in 1952, but his sudden death in January 1953 brought the project to a halt.

Out of respect for the artist, Mrs. Post and her daughter accepted the portrait in its unfinished state. At the time of this writing, the painting hangs at her estate of Hillwood over the mantelpiece in Post's bedroom.

Looking closely at the beautiful portrait, one can discern the results. While the face was finished, other areas, most notably her jewelry and hands, remained incomplete. They had been painted, but not refined by Mr. Candor.

Hillwood Museum describes the portrait as follows:

"The portrait represents Mrs. Merriweather Post in a three-quarter length gown seated on a sofa. Her grey hair is in curls and she wears a décolleté grey dress with a gathered bodice with attached circular motifs. She wears the following jewelry; pearl earrings and an elaborate necklace, an emerald brooch at the center edge of the dress. On her right wrist is a bracelet with an emerald and on her left hand a marquise cut diamond. Her left wrist has another bracelet sketched in. Over her right arm is a lace scarf and under her left arm is an ermine cape which she rests upon.

She holds an orchid in her right hand. The portrait is unfinished because the artist died before he could complete it. The face and upper part are finished but the lower half is only roughly indicated and without details."

Below is a close-up of the detailing on the skirt of Mrs. Merriweather Post's gown.

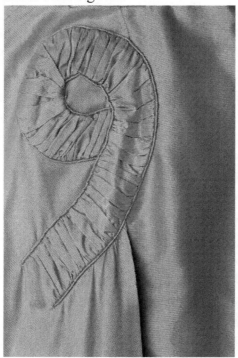

Photos courtesy Hillwood Estate, Museum and Gardens Washington, DC

Chapter 9: Debutants

The Young Ladies Come Out

The postwar years of the late forties, fifties and early sixties saw wealthy Americans embrace the idea of a "coming out" for their daughters. A debutante, when making her debut in society, must look her best for rounds and rounds of parties and dances. This special occasion recognizes them as taking a major step toward some achievement. For young women, that step was toward 'womanhood' and all that the term implied. In the United States, a young girl's debut announced this achievement through glamorous dresses, fancy hairstyles, young men, and dancing the night away.

Each debutante had the official 'coming out' dress and then others for the round of parties she must attend during the season. Just the right gown was important. For many in upper northeastern circles during that time, that meant a dress by Ann Lowe. Ann's layers of flouncy materials or expertly fitting elegant fabrics were just the thing to make the young girls feel confident. One debutante explained that wearing an Ann Lowe gown made her feel beautiful even though she did not see herself as a beauty.

Ann is given credit for designing at least one, perhaps two, debutante dresses for Jacqueline Bouvier in 1947. Just which dress or dresses is unclear although both gowns look like Ann's work. Either I have not been able to verify the accuracy of these statements or I have not been able to obtain permission to use them. Therefore, photos of the gowns are not shown here.

There is no doubt who designed and made the debutant gown worn by Jacqueline's stepsister, Nina Auchincloss.

The photo below shows Nina Auchincloss in an Ann Lowe original at her debut in 1955. Nina and the voluminous pale pink and green tulle gown were featured in an August 1955 edition of *Vogue*. This time, however, Ann was credited in the caption for the photo.

Photo courtesy National Archives and Records Administration.

The caption reads: *"Miss Nina Auchincloss will make her debut this month at a party at "Hammersmith Farms," the Newport house of her father and stepmother, Mr. and Mrs. Hugh Auchincloss. Her pale pink and green tulle dress was made by Ann Lowe."*

In the years following their debut, former debutantes, still in splendid gowns, often attended debutante balls to support the younger girls making their debut. Jackie attended a debutante ball a few years after her own debut in 1952 in a gown attributed to Ann while another gown, worn by Jacqueline's sister, Lee Bouvier (Radzwill) is also attributed to Ann.

Ann and the "American Beauty Gown"

The American Beauty gown, named after the rose of the same name, is silk, tulle, and linen and was designed for Barbara Baldwin Dowd, 1966-67.

Photo Collection this and following page courtesy of Smithsonian National Museum of African American History and Culture, Gift of the Black Fashion Museum founded by Lois K. Alexander-Lane

The American Beauty gown is a museum curator's delight. All the inner seams illustrate Ann's devotion to quality finishing touches. The inner seams are all lined with lace and Ann's desire to have her ladies step in and go is exemplified by the built-in slip and bra.

Bright debutant roses

One striking debutant gown was designed for Ms. Pauline (Polly) Carver Duxbury in 1967. Ann was head designer of The Adam Room at Saks in New York City. Saks and The Adam Room was well known to society ladies. It was there that Polly and Ann worked together to design her one of a kind debutant gown.

The dress is similar to Ann's "The American Beauty," gown because of the wonderful roses gathered on the dress. The dress is silk, tulle, linen, and metal. Hunter green and fuschia floral designs end dramatically in the back. Ann believed that a gown should look as good from the back as the front. This gown was designed for dancing with a low back.

Miss Duxbury was seventeen years old when she wore the dress and she states that the fit is absolutely glorious—*'it's like your skin'*.

The extensive hand work inner construction of the dress has preserved it quite well. Ms. Duxbury says that she still thinks of it as the most beautiful dress in the world.

Photo this and preceding page courtesy of the
National Museum Of American History

"After women, flowers are the most lovely thing God has given the world."

Christian Dior

A debutant from afar

Photo courtesy of debutant, Betty King.

In the photograph above, Ms. Betty King, a descendant of Thomas H. White, founder of the White Sewing Machine Company is pictured in her Ann Lowe debutant gown. She remembers traveling from her hometown of Cleveland, Ohio, to NYC to be fitted for her Ann Lowe original proving that debutants wearing Ann's creation were not just from the major society cities off New York, Boston, and Philadelphia and that it was not unusual for debutantes in cities far removed from New York to travel from their distant hometowns to be personally fitted for their Ann Lowe creations. Young ladies from Dallas, Cincinnati, Pittsburg, and Miami would travel to New York for the Ann Lowe experience.

Ms. King's gown featured an off-the-shoulder neckline and flowers floating around the voluminous skirt.

Beads and Sequins

One debutante gown, this one in white silk organza over white silk taffeta with applied stemmed roses, beads and sequins. Featuring a sweetheart neckline, low back, of-the-shoulder sleeves, fitted natural waist, boned bodice and full bouffant skirt with applied buttercream silk satin stylized foliate padded stems and dimensional rosebuds on the bottom half of the skirt, it was made for dazzling and dancing. Designed and made between 1951 and 1961.

Gown housed at and photo *courtesy of the Museum of the City of New York.* https://www.mcny.org/

Chapter 10: Disasters Coming

Disasters Not Averted

Even as Ann was living her dream she was moving toward disaster. Not just one disaster, but three. They would soon catch up with Ann and change her life forever.

A personal disaster struck in February 1958, Arthur was killed in an automobile accident. Gone was Ann's companion, her only son, her escort to social functions, her business manager. She later stated that she never went to another party for her escort was no longer with her. For years afterward, Ann and Sallie visited his gravesite in Hartsdale, N.Y. monthly.

Arthur's memorial marker at Fernscliff Cemetery and Mausoleum in Hartdale, NY.

Financial disasters always seemed to be nearby. A relative back home in Alabama later said, "*Ann had little business sense.*" Sadly, this description of Ann is borne out by facts.

She charged amazingly low prices for her creations and was often talked into lowering her price even further. She never seemed to consider the difference between what it cost to make the design and what she charged for it. Again, her thoughts were on the joy the gown gave her, not the profit line. After Ann's death her 'adopted daughter', Ruth Alexander, was asked about Ann's financial problems. She explained that Ann "*didn't sew for money. It was the pleasure of making the gown, creating it, that she loved. When she made a gown for $2,000-$3,000.00 she would seldom charge what it was really worth.*"

Additionally, all of her financial arrangements with noted department stores were not in her favor. The stores would make the profit from the sale but because she had to purchase materials needed and pay any employees she had, Ann would barely cover her cost. Many times, she did not cover her cost, thus taking a loss.

While he was alive, her son, Arthur Lee Cohen, who had grown up with her, in and around her shops and around her clients, tried to steady her financial life. Working as her business partner, he helped to keep her business afloat, even as his mother was being talked into reducing her prices. He wanted to keep her business, if not profitable, at least manageable.

With Arthur gone, and given Ann's disinterest in the prices of her creations and in record-keeping, financial problems continued to build, and finally in 1961 disaster struck. The Internal Revenue Service came calling. Ann owed over $12,000 in back taxes and her tax records were incomplete and in disarray. The IRS seized and closed her salon.

At the same time, disaster number three was upon her. While she was living her dream, she was losing her eyesight. In 1962, Ann underwent surgery to remove an eye ruined by glaucoma. Later she developed cataracts in her remaining eye. That eye, however, was saved, but her days as an independent force in the world of fashion were slowly coming to an end.

Two bright notes emerged. One was through a generous anonymous benefactor. When Ann left the hospital after her eye was removed, she learned that her back taxes had been paid in full by an unknown friend. It is believed, that at some point someone had written Jacqueline Kennedy and told her of Ann's plight. There had been no personal response, but Ann felt, upon learning of the anonymous benefactor that it was none other than Jacqueline Kennedy.

There was still, however, a matter of a private debts of $10,000 owed to the many merchants from whom she had purchased expensive fabric over the years. These debts were small in number but owed to many businesses. The owners, however, knew Ann, liked her and her work, and did not push for immediate payment. Eventually, in 1963 she filed for bankruptcy.

Now, unable to maintain her own salon, Ann again went to work for others. For a short time, she worked for Madeleine Couture. It was through this shop that she finally had her first and only fashion show. It was described as a small Champagne affair with the models coming from her clientele.

With her eyesight steadily decreasing, she continued her work for others. From 1961-72 she designed for Saks Fifth Avenue's Adam Room. She also continued to design privately and sold those designs to Neiman Marcus of Dallas, I. Magnum in San Francisco, Henry Bendel, Inc., in New York, and for the Lillian Montaldo chain.

PART III: THE MOST POTOGRAPHED WEDDING DRESS IN AMERICAN HISTORY

Introduction

"I'll never forget it. How could I? Sallie and I were clutching each other's' hands and crying as we sat huddled in front of our small television. She kept whispering soft words of encouragement to me, trying to calm me, but I was inconsolable. She was crying silently; I was gasping for breath and moaning, 'My lady, oh, my lady.'

"Suddenly, I pulled my right hand free of Sallie's grasp and moved my chair closer to the screen. What I saw next made me gasp loudly, and I reached out and ran one finger down the small screen, gently touching the young boy.

Sallie had turned her attention to me when I pulled my hand free, but she quickly turned back to the screen to see what had further distressed me. There she saw what was breaking my heart, that young boy stepping forward and saluting as the caisson carrying the body of his father rolled by. Oh, my lady."

Chapter 11: The Dress Seen 'Round the World

The Dress Seen 'Round the World
Photo credit: Bachrach Getty Images

The 1953 invitation written in Black ink on cream-colored paper simply stated:

Mr. and Mrs. Hugh Dudley Auchincloss
request the honour of your presence
at the marriage of Mrs. Auchincloss' daughter
Jacqueline Lee Bouvier
to
The Honorable John Fitzgerald Kennedy
United State Senate
on Saturday, the twelfth of September
at eleven o'clock
Saint Mary's Church
Spring Street Newport, Rhode Island

It was for this wedding that Ann created 'the dress." The dress that was to become the most photographed wedding dress in American history. The enchanting wedding dress that was designed for the beautiful, young socialite, Jacqueline Bouvier, to wear for her wedding September 12, 1953, as she married John F. Kennedy, then Jr. Senator from Massachusetts.

Ann was well known to Jacqueline Bouvier and her family. She had designed Mrs. Bouvier's wedding dress in 1942 as she married her second husband Hugh D. Auchincloss, and she had designed her mother-of-the-bride dress which she wore for both her daughters' weddings. She also designed elegant gowns for other ladies of the Auchincloss-Bouvier family.

Ann had previously been commissioned to design an earlier wedding gown for Jacqueline Bouvier. It was early 1952 and Jackie was engaged to marry a Wall Street Broker. She met with Ann to discuss her ideas for a wedding dress. When recalling that meeting, Ann remembered that Jackie was very quiet and left with Ann's promise to deliver some sketches at a later date. Before the scheduled appointment arrived, Jackie had broken the engagement.

A year later, when the time came for mother and daughter to consider a design and designer for the upcoming Bouvier-Kennedy society wedding, Janet Auchincloss' thoughts again turned to Ann Lowe. Mrs. Auchincloss, knowing and loving Ann's designs as she did, had confidence that Ann would produce the perfect design for her youngest daughter.

For years it has been reported that Janet Auchincloss wanted her daughter's wedding dress to be an elegant fairy tale ball gown. Those same reports state that Jacqueline wanted something different. She wanted to use her Grandmother Lee's long, expansive rose point Irish lace mantilla paired with a sleek, elegant gown. If reports are to be believed, the young bride wanted sophisticated simplicity, a hallmark of design that the world would later associate with Jacqueline Bouvier Kennedy Onassis. Her mother did not.

An article in the December 12, 1964 issue of *Saturday Evening* Post seems to refute this version of the design of the wedding dress. In that article, Thomas B. Congdon, Jr., quotes Ann as remembering that Jacqueline, when describing what she wanted for her wedding, said she desired *"a tremendous dress…a typical Ann Lowe dress."*

According to that same article, Jackie was considering red for her bridesmaids and asked for Ann's opinion. Ann turned her away from red into the pink that she eventually chose for her bridal party.

For the wedding, the wishes of the mother of the bride, with support from Joe Kennedy, father of the groom, and according to Congdon's article, the desires of the bride, prevailed. Ann won the coveted assignment to design not only a fairy tale gown for a fairy tale wedding but also to design all the dresses to be worn by Jackie's bridal party.

Once her design was accepted, Ann and her assistants worked long hard hours for two months to complete the intricately designed dresses to Ann's level of perfection and her exacting standards were never higher. Her famed finishing touches and care for detail were readily evident in the gown that has become an icon.

The short-sleeved wedding dress was made of fifty yards of ivory silk taffeta. Interwoven bands of tucking formed the figure-hugging bodice which featured a portrait neckline.

It was on the long bouffant skirt that the intricacy of the design stood out. The interwoven bands of tucking were similar to the tucking on the bodice, but here they form large circular designs which floated around the skirt. Below these eye-catching circles the interwoven bands of tucking formed ten waves that encircled the dress and danced as the bride moved. Tiny wax flowers were tucked discreetly around the skirt.

Whether or not the dress was to Jackie's taste, and she later described it as looking like a lampshade, she wore it beautifully on her wedding day. The 600 friends who were invited to the wedding and the additional 700 who were invited to the reception saw only a happy, smiling bride in a beautiful gown that accentuated her figure to perfection.

The dress immediately caught the public's attention

when photographs of Jackie wearing it appeared around the world. The dress was described by many society editors, but the designer's name, with one exception, was never mentioned. Nina Hyde, Social Editor for *The Washington Post,* gave Ann credit in her description of the wedding when she wrote, "the dress was designed by a Negro, Ann Lowe." It was said that the fact that Ann was a Negro pleased her new father-in-law who thought this nod to the 'colored' community would benefit his son in the future.

Then disaster struck. Unknown to anyone in the wedding party was the disaster connected to the dresses. The dresses, after two months of intense work, were finally completed less than two weeks before the wedding date. Ann and her assistants could relax and hope they had captured the essence of what the bride and her mother wanted.

Ten days before the wedding, a water line in Ann's studio broke and spewed gallons of water upon not only the completed bridesmaids' dresses, but also upon the wedding dress. All wedding party garments were ruined.

Ann knew that this commission needed to be completed to perfection for society would learn of the disaster if it were not, and Ann, being a perfectionist, wanted the bridal party to be clothed, not only to the bride and her mother's high expectations but to her own high expectations. Therefore, she allowed only a brief time for crying and soon attacked the problem. She purchased more of the exquisite fabrics and hired extra help to assist her already exhausted staff.

Together they worked day and night to recreate in ten

days what they had spent two months creating. They achieved this seemingly insurmountable task and at the appointed time Ann was able to personally deliver the completed ensemble to the bride and her mother at the family estate.

Ann's niece, Dr. Lenore Cole Alexander, tells the story of Ann arriving at the front door of the estate. She was told to go around to the tradesmen's entrance. Ann is said to have remarked to the person opening the door, "*if I have to enter this by the back door, the bride and bridesmaids will not be dressed for the wedding.*" She was admitted through the front door.

The wedding dress worn with such ease and elegance is now in the John F. Kennedy Presidential Library and Museum in Boston, Ma. It is not on public display at all times. The Library and Museum had the gown restored in 1997, but it is still too delicate to be exposed to the light for long periods.

Jacqueline Bouvier Kennedy, Sept. 12, 1953
Photo Courtesy of Library of Congress

John and Jacqueline Kennedy

Wedding Reception.

Photo from Toni Frissel Collection, Courtesy Library of Congress

For Ann, who loved her designs, the worldwide praise for her designs must have buoyed her spirit, but the assignment and commission did nothing to lift her bank account. That aspect of this wedding remained a disaster for Ann.

The wedding dress cost $500.00 in 1953. Ann, by the time she purchased the fabrics, paid the rent on her studio, and paid her assistants, expected to realize a $700.00 profit from the entire wedding commission.

That was before the water disaster.

After purchasing additional fabrics, hiring extra help, and requiring overtime from everyone, all profit disappeared. In its place, Ann suffered a $2,000.00 loss. She never mentioned the disaster to the Auchincloss, Bouvier, or Kennedy families, but in time it was known to all concerned parties. *Photo below courtesy of the Library of Congress, Public Domain.*

Photo from Toni Frissel Collection, Courtesy Library of Congress

Photo from Toni Frissel Collection, Courtesy Library of Congress

Unknown to many was the fact that Ann had been asked to maintain confidentiality before designing the dresses for the Bouvier-Kennedy wedding party. Although he was years from the presidency, John Kennedy was already an important member of the U.S. Senate and his party. His family had big plans for him, so confidentiality, not trading upon their name for recognition of your own, was important. Ann liked Jacqueline and enjoyed talking and working with her and willingly agreed. Thus, should Ann ever wish to publicize her role in the wedding, the bride would have to approve of what was written.

In the back of her mind, Ann thought this confidentiality agreement would cover anything written by anyone about the Bouvier Kennedy wedding, especially after Jacqueline became First Lady. Therefore, Ann was hurt when an April 1961 *Ladies Home Journal* characterized Ann as a "*colored woman dressmaker, not the haute couture.*" Her hurt feelings led Ann to write the First Lady on April 5, 1961.

In part, she said, "*Dear Mrs. Kennedy: The reason for writing this note is to tell you how hurt I feel as a result of an article, the last of a series, about you in the Ladies Home Journal in which the reporter stated your wedding gown was by a 'colored woman dressmaker, not the haute couture.' I realize it was not intentional on your part but as you once asked me not to release any publicity without your approval, I assume that the article in question, and others, was passed by you.*
You know I have never sought publicity but I would prefer to be referred to as a 'noted Negro designer,' which in every sense I am. My name does not need to be

mentioned as many of my socially prominent customers know I did your wedding as I have your wedding portrait in my studio."

The response from the White House came just five days later when Mrs. Kennedy's secretary called Ann assuring her that Mrs. Kennedy did not see the final text of the article before publication. Thus, she had no way of knowing in advance that Ann was referred to in that manner. Even though Ann would have liked a retraction or correction and the White House apparently tried to get one, one never came. Still, Ann held no animosity toward the Kennedys.

The photo on the following page clearly shows some of the design insight and skill that went into the wedding dress that Jacqueline wore so beautifully.

Replica of the dress on display at the John F. Kennedy
Presidential Library, Boston MA. .
*Photo courtesy of the John F. Kennedy Presidential Library,
Boston, Massachusetts*

Recognition Fifty Years Later

Fifty years after the famed wedding, the world had seen horrors not imagined earlier and both the bride and groom were no longer living. There was a celebration, however, of that momentous event 50 years earlier. In the news release announcing the celebration, one sees that Ann Lowe is now receiving her long overdue recognition as the designer.

News Release

Special Exhibit Celebrates 50th Anniversary of the Wedding of Jacqueline Bouvier and John F. Kennedy

For Immediate Release: April 23, 2003 BOSTON—On May 15, 2003, the John F. Kennedy Library and Museum will open a special exhibit to celebrate the 50th anniversary of the September 12, 1953, wedding of Jacqueline Bouvier and John Fitzgerald Kennedy. The Museum exhibit will run through October 31, 2003.

Highlights of the exhibit include:

Mrs. Kennedy's ivory-silk-taffeta wedding dress, designed by African-American fashion-designer Ann Lowe.

PART IV: ANN'S STUDIO
CREATING MAGIC

"All the pleasure I have had, I owe to my sewing.
I enjoy it so much; I wish I were physically able to
do all the work myself."

Ann Lowe

Chapter 12: Floral Wonders
Portfolio II

Designing with Flowers

Permission to use photo given to the author *courtesy of Mrs. Patricia Penrose Schieffer* 1959:

Ann designed the gown shown on the preceding page for the Adam Room of Saks Fifth Avenue. It was worn by Ms. Patricia Penrose, who later became the wife of Bob Schieffer, a noted American television newscaster. She wore it to the Steeplechase Ball, Fort Worth, in 1959. The gown is a full-length, shades of pink satin with an inset of pink organza on the front and bodice. Scattered flowers with rhinestones adorn the gown. The photo on the preceding page shows the final effect as Ann wanted it with the petticoats she designed to go with the gown.

Photos this page and the preceding page, *courtesy of Collection of the Smithsonian National Museum of African American History and Culture, Gift of the Black Fashion Museum founded by Lois K. Alexander*-Lane

Embroidered Flowers

Permission to use photo given to the author *courtesy
of Mrs. Patricia Penrose Schieffer*

Also from 1958 comes this cream silk faille dress with Ann's floral applique emphasizing the neckline and waist. The silk and linen of the dress combine to give it the strength and shaping needed for the bodice. The dress features a scoop neckline in front and a deep scoop neckline in back. Small, cap sleeves are featured.

*Photo this page and preceding page courtesy of
Collection of the Smithsonian National Museum of
African American History and Culture, Gift of the Black
Fashion Museum founded by Lois K. Alexander-Lane*

Looking at the photo on the preceding pages, we can again see the effect a petticoat or hoop has on the wide skirts Ann loved to make.

The Embroidered cream and pink flowers with green leaves provide evidence of Ann's love of flowers and embroidery. The embroidery here, however, is machine embroidery, a departure from Ann's hand sewing. Perhaps time was of the essence and there was no time for the handwork. Perhaps, but we have no way of knowing. The embroidery was sewn as separate items and then stitched to the dress where needed. There are six sprays of flowers sewn onto the skirt. Two lengths of cream silk faille are pleated and attached at the back waist to create streamers that reach to the hemline of the skirt.

The interior of the dress shows Ann's expectation of excellence even on the inside of her garments. There is boning in the front and back of the bodice for support, and there are individual breast cups sewn into the garment for extra support. An interior waistband of cream grosgrain ribbon is tacked to the interior waistline and closes at the center back.

The interior of the skirt is unlined and but it has one petticoat. The petticoat is made of a cream faille lined with heavy linen. Using one of Ann's favorite designs, the petticoat is hemmed with ruched cream tulle and edged with stiffener. It attaches to the waist at the center back with a hook-and-eye and a metal snap.

While there is no label in the dress, it was made for the same young lady as the previous dress and features not only her desired features but also shows Ann's characteristic design and finishing techniques. The authenticity of the dress has been verified by the owner and the Black Fashion History Museum created by Lois Alexander. Additionally, both dresses were gifted to the Smithsonian by the same woman.

Floral Fantasy

The evening gown below, a soft gray with blue flowers, from 1956, is silk, cotton, and glass (the small rhinestones). The colors of the gown and the use of flowers and lace are apparent in the second photo.

Photos courtesy of the Metropolitan Museum of Art: Gift of Mrs. J. Winston Fowlkes and Mrs. Will R. Gregg, Accession Number: 1979.151 www.metmuseum.org

Something Similar

A very similar dress from 1962, while darker in color, also features Ann's use of floral embellishment. This gown is possibly for the same client as the previous gown for the benefactors of the dress to the museum are the same.

Photo courtesy of the Metropolitan Museum of Art: Gift of Mrs. J. Winston Fowlkes and Mrs. Will R. Gregg www.metmuseum.org

Short and Sassy

For a complete change, a short, sweet day dress designed by Ann in the mid-to-late 1950s

The simplicity of this dress belies the hours of intricate hand-sewing involved to achieve the built-in bra and the exact

fit of the dress. Additionally, there were hundreds of individual flowers which accentuated the original lacy fabric of the dress.

Photos courtesy of Metropolitan Museum of Art, Gift of Dr. and Mrs. Samuel A. Thompson, 1981. Accession Number 1981.89 www.metmuseum.org

Colorful Magic

A 1962-64 colorful evening gown of silk produced while Ann was the designer working for Saks Fifth Avenue's Adam Room.

*Photos this page and the previous courtesy of
Metropolitan Museum of Art. Gift of Mrs. Carl Tucker,
Jr. 1979. Accession Number 1979.260
www.metmuseum.org*

Designing for the Opera

At the age of 67, under her own name for A.F. Chantilly, Ann created this Italian silk and cotton opera gown and coat.

*Photos this page and previous courtesy of Metropolitan
Museum of Art: Gift of Florence J. Cowell, 1980 Accession
Number: 1980 433.2 www.metmuseum.org*

From Ebony Magazine through Huffington Post:
http://www.huffingtonpost.com/2013/02/05/ann-lowe-
Black-fashion-designer-

Ann, in 1966, with London model Judith Guile
modeling the opera dress described on previous pages,.
It is showing as a slightly different shade of blue due to
film processing. Photo taken in Ann's studio with photo
of Jacqueline Kennedy in the background

From the inside of the opera gown.

I spoke with Ann's model for the opera gown, Ms. Judith Guile (Palmer) and then listened to her BBC interview. She warmly remembered Ann as being "very, very, slim, beautifully spoken, and always very gracious."

Ann took the time to teach Judith to make the time-consuming fabric flowers she loved. They were made in ordered steps with a beautiful finished flower or bud which would then be sewn onto the garment.

Ms. Guile recalled the large black hats and the black clothing Ann favored for herself. She explained that she enjoyed working with Ann because Ann had a sweet, calming nature.

Something Different

Phot os courtesy of Metropolitan Museum of Art Gift of Florence J. Cowell, Accession Number 1980. 433 www.metmuseum.org

A Few More Flowers

1960 evening gown: nylon, metallic thread and silk.

Photo courtesy of Metropolitan Museum of Art: Gift of Lucy Curley Joyce Brennen. Accession Number:1979.144 www.metmuseum.org

Wedding Sophistication

Miss Ann Bellah on her wedding day in 1964.

Photo courtesy of Ann Bellah Copeland

Manhattan socialite Ann Power Bellah was fortunate enough to have two Ann Lowe designs. The first was for her coming-out and the second for her wedding.

While speaking about her wedding gown, Mrs. Ann Bellah Copeland recently explained her choice of Ann as her designer.

"As Ann had made my coming-out dress, I wanted her to do my wedding dress as I knew she would understand the concept that I wanted. I was extremely tired of frilly, flouncy full-skirted wedding dresses. I wanted something very simple and serene with a court train. She was able to give me exactly what I wanted."

Together Ann and the bride designed a dress that was truly unique. It featured a long court train that fell from her shoulders down the full length of the ivory silk faille gown. Reflecting the bride's desires, the dress featured no ornamentation, showcasing instead the sophistication of the gown and the beauty of the DuPont wedding veil which the bride wore at the request of the groom. The dress and the veil perfectly complimented each other.

The outward appearance of the dress, however, is the only change Ann made during this commission. Ann still maintained the high quality, the expert cutting, and the special finishing touches for which she was known. One of the finishing touches that would not be seen by the public but which Ann insisted on, was the lacy trimming of the inside seams. As always, Ann believed that it was in this type of finishing that ensured a perfect fit.

The bride considered having Ann design and make her eight bridesmaids' dresses also, but learned that such a commission might be too much for Ann's health at that time.

"In the end, it was just my dress and I was very, very happy with it," explained Mrs. Bellah Copeland.

Miss Bellah wore the dress June 6, 1964, when she wed Gerret Copeland, the son of Lamont du Pont Copeland, the president of the Du Pont Company at the time.

Expressing her thoughts about Ann Lowe and her place in design history, Mrs. Bellah Copeland added,

"Ann was a lovely, gentle lady. Had she been designing today, she would be considered one of the great designers. Her time in history was against her.

Something Slightly Different

A different type evening dress is this 1956 silk. Color variations observed in the photos are due to the age of the photographs and the lighting. Would love to see it with its underskirt/slip.

Photos courtesy of Metropolitan Museum of Art. Gift of Sarnia Hayes Hoyt. Accession Number: 1994.562.of Art. www.metmuseum.org

145

Chapter 13: Everyday Affairs

Ann and the Media with Mike Douglas

The very popular *Mike Douglas Show* originated in
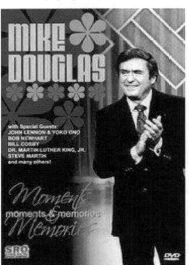
Cleveland, Ohio in 1961, but was seen in nationwide syndication and from 1963 until 1981. The program was aimed at the housewives of America and was soon a favorite afternoon talk show with a large viewing audience. Mike was a gracious host and his guests were the movie and television stars, favorite musicians, and authors of the time. It was the era of new the consciousness of the Civil Rights movement, and Mike always tried to be relevant.

It was in the mid-sixties, December 22, 1964, to be exact, that designer Ann Lowe appeared on the Emmy Award winning show. By that time the show was broadcast through 150 markets across the country, thus introducing Ann to thousands.

After discussing her career and seeing several of her gowns, Mike asked Ann to explain the driving force behind her work. She explained that it was not a quest for fame or fortune but a desire *"to prove that a Negro can become a major dress designer."*

From a newspaper of the 1960s

"MIKE DOUGLAS SHOW" Miss Lowe, designer and creator of Jacque Bouvier Kennedy's wedding gown bro a collection of her "one-of-a-kind" go

After the Mike Douglas show, Ann continued to attract the elite of society, and she continued to choose her clients as strictly as they chose her. She was proud of her past accomplishments and proudly displayed photographs of her former clients and designs in her studio. Along the way, Ann was labeled by one reporter as the *"Dean of American Designers."*

In 1965 she again opened her own shop, "Ann Lowe Originals," on prestigious Madison Avenue in New York City. Later Calvin Klein would house one of his design studios on the second floor of the same building.

In 1966 Ann was listed in the directory *Who's Who of American Women.* Also, in 1966, along with many of her clients, Ann was listed in the *National Society Directory.*

Ann and Advertising

Before Long, Ann's fame was enough to convince her employers to use her in advertising. At one point, Saks Fifth Avenue proudly announced that they were the exclusive salon for Ann Lowe creations. The announcement, complete with a silhouette of Ann read as follows:

Saks Fifth Avenue
Takes Pride in Announcing
that the
Debut and Bridal Gown
Collection
created by
Ann Lowe
can now be found
exclusively in
The Adams Room

In another ad, in the Park Avenue Social Review, they featured a model proudly wearing an Ann Lowe original.

An Unusual Assignment

In the 1960s, with her eyesight failing and her bank account shrinking, Ann was commissioned by Baron Walter Langer von Langendorff, of the Evyan Perfume Company, makers of White Shoulders, Timeless, and Jungle Gardenia, not to design gowns, but to replicate miniature gowns of the inaugural ball gowns of some of America's First Ladies. While the original full-size gowns were already on display in the Smithsonian Institution's First Ladies gown collection, the sets of Ann's miniature gowns were made to be displayed in major department stores throughout the country to promote two of Evyan's perfumes, "White Shoulders" and "Great Lady."

In 2005, twenty-eight of the miniature gowns were donated to the National First Ladies' Library in Canton, Ohio. Because of the fragility of the gowns, they require special care and are not always on open display, but when they are, they are displayed in the order of the presidential administrations.

While Ann was not the original designer of these gowns, she did insist on maintaining her exacting standards of fine craftsmanship as she remade them in miniature. A representative of the museum believes that this dedication to excellence enabled Ann's miniature replicas to stand the test of time better than some of the gowns which were reproduced by others. Her expectation of precise inside finishes and fine needlework kept them in top form as the years passed.

These forty-one inch replicas are extremely popular with guests at the First Ladies' Library and the staff strives to always have three of them on exhibit at a time while the remaining dresses 'rest' to preserve the delicate fabric. The originals for which Ann made the replicas were worn by Mrs. Pat Nixon, wife of President Richard Nixon, Mrs. Grace Collidge, wife of President Calvin Coolidge, and Mrs. Helen Taft, wife of President Howard Taft.

Pat Nixon's
Mini Inaugural Gown

Grace Collidge's
Mini Inaugural Gown

Photos courtesy of the National First Ladies' Library, Canton, Ohio.

Helen Taft's Mini Inaugural Gown
Photo courtesy of the National First Ladies' Library, Canton, Ohio.

"Every Woman is a Princess."
Christian Dior

Chapter 14: AK-SAR-BEN

Phyllis Dalkhe wearing her 1961 AK SAR BEN Court
Dress. "My Cinderella Dress."
Photo Courtesy of Phyllis Fonda Dalkhe

For the Queen and her Court

Most people outside of Nebraska have never heard of AK-SAR-BEN, Nebraska spelled backward. Perhaps Ann Lowe would have been counted in that number in early 1961 while she was working as a featured designer in the couture Adam Room boutique at Saks Fifth Avenue. She would soon learn of the importance of AK-SAR-BEN and she would play an important part in the 1961 celebration that surrounded the yearly event.

Founded in 1895 by a group of prominent Omaha, Nebraska businessmen as a means to keep the Nebraska State Fair in Omaha, the committee grew into a major philanthropic organization, not only in Nebraska but throughout the heartland of America.

As with many social/philanthropic organizations AK-SAR-BEN sponsors an annual Coronation and Scholarship Ball which promotes and celebrates volunteerism, philanthropy, and community by providing over 50 scholarships each year to deserving students in Nebraska and western Iowa.

Each year, for its annual coronation ball, the Knights of AK-SAR-BEN commission a top fashion designer to create gowns for its princesses and countesses. Ann's flair for elegant entrance gowns and her position with the Adam Room at Saks Fifth Avenue made her the perfect choice for the 1961 event.

The ball committee always chose the designer and dictated the color scheme for each year's ball. Ann's colors were to be shades of Flamingo rose and silver. Her designs had to be submitted to the committee for they knew the look they wanted for their ball. Big, elegant

155

gowns, flowing skirts, and yards and yards of fabric were what they wanted.

With Ann as the designer, that is what they received. She produced six designs for the many princesses and made these in varying shades of pink. Yards and yards of tulle, hand beading, sequins, rhinestones, and Ann's ever present delicate flowers embellished each gown.

Once again, Ann had been called upon to design gowns in the larger-than-life- billowing style she loved. The results were amazing. Following her usual desire for perfection, Ann insisted upon labor-intensive techniques to create the individually hand-beaded embellishments for the gowns she designed. The detailed flourishes on the exquisite queen's gown and the 24 countesses and princesses AK-SAR-BEN gowns took dozens of hours of hand sewn labor for each gown. The seamstresses hired by Ann worked long hard days to fulfill her exacting expectations.

For participants in the 1961 AK-SAR-BEN coronation ball, the results were unforgettable. For the mid-westerners who could not be at the event, Marilyn Russum of the *Omaha World Herald* provided an in-depth description of the event. She described the four shades of pink found in gowns as petal, hyacinth, begonia, and camellia. She enthusiastically described the French nylon tulle as twelve layers of fabric used in the skirts. Just in case they were not full enough, these 12 layers were worn over hoops. The pressers, she stated, needed two hours to press each dress. The dresses had trains and hand-sewn jewels. There were many flowers adorning these special Ann creations.

The queen wore white. It has been said that the 1961

queen's gown had hundreds of yards of white French netting in twelve layers of net hand-embroidered in 60 different motifs with silver and crystal bugle beads, snowflakes, pearls, and cut-crystal pendants forming voluminous skirts. Again from the *Omaha World Herald* comes a description of this dress as *"dewdrops on French Net."* Although it fit the queen perfectly, it was extremely unwieldy as she tried to perform her duties. Even dancing was very difficult.

1961 AK-SAR-BEN Queen, Connie O'Neal.
Photo used courtesy of Connie O'Neil

Another1961 AK-SAR-BEN beauty, Ann Jessop, is shown wearing one of the gowns Ann Lowe designed for the 1961 Court.

Photo courtesy of Ann Jessop.
1961 Aksarben Court

Chapter 15: Ann's Magic Portfolio III

Cotton and Silk 1968

This 1968 cotton and silk gown, housed at the Metropolitan Museum of Art, is very similar to Ann's American Beauty Rose gown. While similar to the American Beauty gown, the flowers, and details are different from the previous gown. As the label indicates, the gown was designed while Ann was working for A.F. Chantilly. Again, the low back allows for dancing without the lady's partner's hands touching the dress. Ann wanted beautiful backs for her gowns but did not want sweaty hands marring her creations. The gown is not on public view.

Photos for cotton and silk this page and the previous courtesy of Metropolitan Museum of Art Gift of Florence J. Cowell, Accession Number 1980. 433.3 www.metmuseum.org

Black with Pink Rose, Green Sash

From 1960, silk, chiffon, and taffeta with netting.

Photo courtesy of the Collection of the Smithsonian National Museum of African-American History and Culture, gift of the Black Fashion Museum founded by Lois K. Alexander Lane.

Field of Red Flowers

From the Cincinnati Art Museum come three beautiful Ann Lowe dresses beginning with a red flowered design guaranteed to catch the eye, *Dress and Belt, 1930–1934 in silk.*

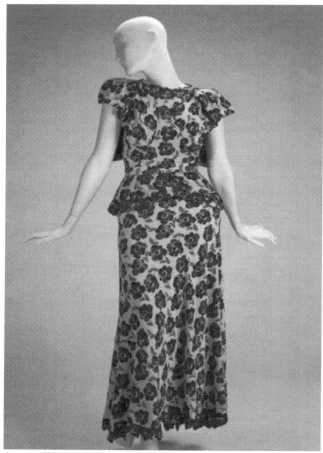

Ann Lowe (American, 1898–1981), *Dress and Belt*, 1930–34, silk, https://www.cincinnatiartmuseum.org/ Anonymous Gift, 1999.810a-b

The dress features a n interesting flirty back design just made for dancing!

Ann Lowe (American, 1898–1981), *Dress and Belt*, 1930–34, silk, https://www.cincinnatiartmuseum.org/ Anonymous Gift, 1999.810a-b

Blue and White

White flowers on a field of blue: Dress with a
jacket and a barely discernable belt.

Ann Lowe (American, 1898–1981), *Dress, Jacket, and
Belt*, 1930–35, silk, sequins,
https://cincinnatiartmuseum.org/ Anonymous Gift,
1999.812a-c

A Little Something Different In Silk

Ann's trademark use of flowers is shown here, not as hand-created accessories, but imprinted on silk. The flower is a Japanese version of the Chrysanthemum.

Ann Lowe (American, 1898–1981), *Dress and Belt*, 1935–38, silk, https://cincinnatiartmuseum.org/ Anonymous Gift, 1999.811a-b

Elegant Teal Blue

Teal blue floral brocade dress and cropped jacket
Florence Colgate Rumbough Trevor. The dress features
silk satin with all over brocaded medium-scale design of
scattered flowers with leaves and stems in pink, blue,
copper, and green.

. Gift of the Black Fashion Museum founded by Lois K.
Alexander-Lane *Courtesy of Smithsonian National
Museum African American History and Culture*

Unusual Source Authentication:
A Red and White Ball Gown

The other gowns and day dresses found in this book have been authenticated by museums across the country or by their owners. The following gown is somewhat different.

Estate sales and museum deaccessions, the removal of an item from a museum or art gallery in order to sell it to raise funds, offer auction houses the opportunity to have hidden jewels in their catalogs. The Charles A. Whitaker Auction Company often hosts specialty vintage clothing and textile auctions. The auction house has verified that this is an Ann Lowe gown. When it was auctioned, the selling price surpassed the estimated price.

From the 1950s comes this one-of-a-kind gown. White tulle with appliqued red velvet trim decorate the voluminous layered skirt. There is an interior corset for shaping and a large stiff underskirt. The applicate bows around the bottom or oversized. The gown has fitted cap sleeves. All of the other gowns and day dresses found in this book have been authenticated by museums across the country. The following gown is somewhat different.

Red and White Ball Gown is simplicity with a strong dash of color at its best.

Photo this page and following courtesy of Whitaker Auctions

The auction house was able to acquire the gown through deaccession, the selling of a piece of art by a museum in order to raise money for the museum.

Ann's Swan Song

One of Ann's most meaningful designs, another
wedding dress, was commissioned in 1968 when Ann was
almost 70 years old. While her eyesight was diminished
by this time, her brilliant artistic mind was as strong as
ever. The result was a spectacular wedding dress for a
special young woman.

Since the 1940's Ann had been friends with Dr. and
Mrs. Robert Mance Jr. and their family. Dr. Mance was a
vice president of the general board of the National
Council of Churches and financial secretary of the
A.M.E. Church. The Mance's daughter, Elizabeth,
graduated from the Oberlin Conservatory of Music in
Ohio. She became a concert pianist and at some of her
piano recitals she wore gowns created for her by Ann.

In 1968, after study at the Royal Conservatory of
Music in Brussels, Elizabeth became engaged. She and
her mother began planning Elizabeth's society wedding.
Their designer of choice for her wedding dress was, of
course, Ann Lowe.

Since this young lady and her family were important
to Ann, the occasion of her wedding became very special
to Ann. Through the years Ann had designed and sewn
for a few members of her own race. She wore her own
designs with style and elegance and sent fashions back to
her family members, many still in Alabama. Elizabeth's
wedding dress, however, may be the first wedding dress
Ann designed for a high society member of her own race.
Additionally, Ann designed and made all the dresses for
the large wedding party. On the day of the wedding, Ann
was in attendance, wearing her signature hat, to observe

the beauty she had helped create.

The wedding gown, made of lace imported from Switzerland, featured sheer long sleeves, delicate flowers around the portrait neckline, and a long billowing train of lace. The train fell from a headpiece designed with lace flowers designed by Ann and sewn into Elizabeth's hair. Matching flowers were hand sewn onto the five yards of the train.

The Mance wedding dress was special to Ann for another reason; she knew her designing days were drawing to an end. With her failing eyesight and with frailty slowing her down, the dress became known as Ann's "Swan Song."

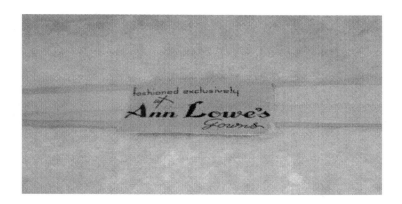

PART V:
REMEMBERING ANN

Chapter 16: The Later Years

The End Nears

Ann often said that sewing was the thing that gave her the most pleasure in her life. She stated that she wished she could do all the sewing herself implying that she did not like to rely on her assistants. Nevertheless, the volume of her output, the demands for perfection she placed upon herself, and her failing eyesight meant that Ann had to rely on others.

It was at this time that Sallie, who had been living with Ann for years, became a valuable assistant to her younger sister not only in the fashion industry but in all aspects of life. Ann, however, never completely gave over the reins of her business and rested on her laurels. As she aged, she continued to keep her establishment open even though she did very little of the actual sewing herself. Her designs were still from her brilliant mind, but they were dictated to staff members who drew them to her exacting expectations and executed them to perfection. Sallie was on hand to hear the details and descriptions flow from Ann's artistic mind and to see if they were interpreted as she felt her sister meant them to be.

They continued in this fashion for several years. Since Ann was sharing her Harlem apartment home with Sallie, the dependence on the older sister came naturally. After any time spent working, Sallie became Ann's strength and caregiver at night. In a December 1966 article in Ebony Magazine, the sisters stated that Ann would go to her studio for the day then return home to go to bed immediately. There she ate her dinner, talked with

Sallie, and continued to design in her head. She would take a warm bath, then back to bed while Sallie often read the daily newspaper to Ann. The frailty and ever diminishing eyesight were taking their toll.

This was the working arrangement until 1967 when Sallie died. Her death announcement in the *New York Times* identified her as "Sallie Mathis of Saks Fifth Avenue, Sister of Ann Lowe." After Sallie's death, Ann had to rely on family members, assistants, and friends to do for her the things Sallie had always done.

Ann retired from her beloved career in 1972 and continued living in her familiar Harlem ground floor apartment for as long as possible. She had lived there for over 30 years, but finally she and all who loved her were forced to admit that she needed constant care.

In August 1976, Ann was to be honored by the Alpha Phi Alpha International Fraternity at their 70th Anniversary convention in Rockefeller Center, NYC. The Alpha wives of Greater New York hosted a luncheon. The honoree was to be Ann Lowe.

Two days before the luncheon, Ann suffered a cardiac event and was hospitalized. She was not able to be present to hear the words honoring her, nor the applause from the room full of admiring women as young women modeled several of her gowns.

Present in her place was her granddaughter Audrey Lowe Hassell, Arthur's daughter. Also present was Audrey's daughter, Ann's great-granddaughter. She accepted the plaque that the organization had prepared for Ann. After the ceremony, the plaque was presented to Ann in the hospital. Almost blind by that time, she had to appreciate the evidence of the group's admiration of her talented mind and nimble fingers by running those same fingers slowly over the plaque.

Acknowledging that her eyesight had failed her, Ann responded, *"There are still a thousand ideas for dresses in my mind, dresses which I see in great detail."*

Also present at the luncheon was Ruth Williams Alexander, the daughter of Ann's closest friend in Tampa. After Ruth's mother died, she lived with Ann for a time. Throughout the New York years, Ruth was nearby as a friend and companion for Ann. After Sallie died, Ann could not live alone. Ruth was there for her. When Ann moved from her Harlem apartment she moved into Ruth's home where she spent her final years as part of Ruth's family. This devotion earned Ruth the title of 'daughter' or 'adopted daughter.' She was there for Ann until the end of her remarkable life which came on February 25, 1981 at the age of 83.

Her funeral, described as a quiet and dignified Harlem funeral, was held at St. Mark's United Methodist Church, Manhattan. It is said that the final services were paid for by her friend and benefactor Baron Von Landendorff of the Evyan Perfume Company.

Epilogue

"Elegance is not standing out, but being remembered."
Christian Dior

For 82 years Ann Cole Lowe made her mark upon this earth. In Alabama she is remembered as Ann Cole, daughter, cousin, and aunty who left behind a legacy. In the fashion world of NY and beyond she is remembered as Ann Lowe, couturier to wealthy society women of her time. There, too, she left a legacy.

To all who knew her she is remembered as a trailblazer who knew what she wanted to do with her life and lived and worked tirelessly to fulfill that dream. To young ladies who come after her, she should be a role model. Ann proved beyond a doubt that *"a Negro can become a major dress designer."*

Ann Cole Lowe 1898-1981

Photo courtesy of Clara Harvey,
Great-Granddaughter of Ann Cole Lowe

Obituary: From the New York Times, March 1, 1981

ANN LOWE, 82, DESIGNED GOWNS FOR EXCLUSIVE CLIENTELE IN SOCIETY

By TIMOTHY M. PHELPS

Published: March 1, 1981

Ann Lowe, who designed gowns for debutantes and society brides, including the gown Jacqueline Bouvier wore when she married Senator John F. Kennedy, died last Wednesday after a long illness in the Queens home of her daughter, where she had lived for the last five years. She was 82 years old.

The gown the future First Lady wore for her marriage in 1953 in Newport, R.I., was described as one "of silk taffeta, with a fitted bodice embellished with interwoven bands of tucking, finished with a portrait neckline and a bouffant skirt."

But although her products were described in detail in the society pages, Mrs. Lowe was "society's best-kept secret," according to a magazine portrait of her in 1964.

According to the article in The Saturday Evening Post, the matrons of the country's leading families, including the du Ponts, Lodges, Auchinclosses and Hamiltons, passed Mrs. Lowe's name from generation to generation.

An Exclusive Clientele

She charged what was then a lot of money for a dress - $500 for the Kennedy gown - but her clients were sometimes able to talk down her prices, so that, after paying her seamstresses, she often lost money, according to the magazine article. Seventeen years ago, at the height of her career, she was said to be almost penniless.

Mrs. Lowe was determined to work for only the best families. "I've been as careful about the people I work for as any social climber," she told the magazine. "I don't do many dresses, so I have to be selective."

Mrs. Lowe was born in Grayton , Ala. She was the daughter of a dressmaker and was educated in Montgomery at the S.T. Taylor Design School. She married Lee Cohen. Their son, Arthur Lee, was her partner in business until his death in 1958.

She came to New York in 1928 and worked for various salons and the Saks Fifth Avenue department store, opening her own Madison Avenue shop, Ann Lowe Originals, in 1968. Her dresses were all originals, never mass-produced. Five of her designs are in the costume institute of the Metropolitan Museum of Art.

In addition to her adopted daughter, Ruth Alexander, Mrs. Lowe is survived by a granddaughter and two great grandchildren. Her funeral will be Tuesday at St. Marks United Methodist Church, 138th Street and Edgecombe Avenue, Manhattan.

Note: Both the name of Ann's hometown and the Taylor School of Design are incorrectly stated. This obituary appeared in several newspapers across the U.S.

This is the full memorial marker honoring Ann and her son Arthur at Fernscliff Cemetery and Mausoleum in Hartdale, Westchester County, N.Y.

Remembering Ann
What others said about her

"She was always beautifully dressed in black with large hats." Judith Guile, former Ann Lowe model to the author. 2020

"Some of the pictures that you see of Chanel, I...I think of Ann Lowe, that sort of simple elegant...different colored skin, a lady beautifully dressed with a hat, who was making clothes." Betty King, Debutant, to the author. 1916

"Ann was a lovely, gentle lady. Had she been designing today, she would be considered one of the great designers. Her time in history was against her." Ann Bellah Copeland. Bride, to the author. 2016

"Rich women pass her name among themselves; some even had her designs copied; some even cheated her." Thomas B. Congdon, Saturday Evening Post, 1966

"Ann Lowe is creating art...Dresses are her art, and nobody these days want to pay for it." Arthur Dages, Fine Fabrics Importer

"Everything is so perfect—and she didn't charge enough for the cost of the fabrics or the handwork that went into them." Nancy Davis, a curator at the National Museum of History.

"Lowe is an expert in her field who has been turning out impeccably dressed debutantes for twenty years, and charges up to $500 for her custom-made evening stunners." 1957 the New York Times

"Ann didn't sew for money. It was the pleasure of making the gown, creating it, that she loved. When she made a gown for $2,000-$3,000.00 she would seldom charge what it was really worth." Ruth Alexander, adopted daughter.

"She wasn't the sort of person that would bend over backward, or charmed to make them buy her clothes. She didn't need to do that." Judith Guile, former Ann Lowe Model

"This was definitely my Cinderella gown." Phyllis Fonda Dahlke, Aksarben, to the author, 2016.

"She deals in elegance, and that's an idea that has been forgotten in this country---flamboyance has replaced it. She's the only person left who has the courage to continue along these lines." Arthur Dages, Fine Fabrics Importer.

"Sewing was her lifeblood. It was her gift, but also her being. She just wanted to sew. She just wanted to make beautiful dresses that gave her clients joy." Nancy Davis, a curator at the National Museum of History

"There was never anyone like Annie." Sarah Keller Hobbs, 1934 Gasparilla queen, Tampa Tribune

"She was beautifully spoken and very dignified." Judith Guile, former Ann Lowe, model, to the author. 2020

"I was fortunate to have met Ms. Lowe during one of my fittings at the Adam Room. She was very gracious and attentive. I know what a privilege it was to have worn these exquisite gowns." Patricia Penrose Schieffer, 2021

Photo courtesy of NAARA:
flickr/http://www.flicks.com/photos/usnationalarchives

Ann, in her own words

"I like for my dresses to be admired. I like to hear about it---the ooohs and ahhs as they come into the ballroom. Like when someone tells me 'the Ann Lowe dresses were doing all the dancing at the cotillion last night.' That's what I like to hear." Thomas B. Congdon, *Saturday Evening Post, 1964*

"I love my clothes and I'm particular about whom I sew for. I'm an awful snob. I'm not interested in sewing for café society or for social climbers. I do not cater to Mary and Sue. I sew for the families of the social register." Ebony Magazine, *December 1966, Gerri Major.*

"I feel so happy when I am making clothes that I could just jump up and down with joy." Oakland Tribune

"For twenty years I worked for others. I rode one person after another to glory on my back."

"I just knew that if I could come to New York and make dresses for society people my dreams would be fulfilled." 1966 Oakland Tribune

"He wanted a real wife, not someone who was forever jumping out of bed to sketch."

"There are still a thousand ideas for dresses in my mind, dresses which I see in great detail."

"All the pleasure I have had, I owe to my sewing. I enjoy it so much, I wish I were physically able to do all the work myself." Ebony Magazine, December 1966, Gerri Major.

Chapter 17: Ann in today's world

In Film and Theatre

Interestingly enough, for an artist who was unknown to the mainstream in her day, Ann and her work can be found in several places and mediums in modern American Culture. From three media columns in 1915 when I first researched Ann until 2021, the amount of print space devoted to Ann quadrupled in number. This year, 2021, Ann's story is everywhere.

The first edition of this book, *Something to Prove*, has been picked up by a major U.S. film company and also by a U.K. theatrical group. Ann is no longer "Society's Best Kept Secret."

In historic magazines...

Author's collection of historic magazines featuring Ann Lowe

Local newspapers…

Tallahassee Democrat, March 2016

Tampa Tribune, August 7, 1976

From Dothan, Alabama.

Lewis Chapter DAR honors late fashion designer

- BY PENNY CARTER
- Feb 14, 2018 Updated Jul 15, 2020

Despite living most of her life outside of Barbour County, Lowe will remain one of the county's treasures and always a native to the area. It was with this in mind that members of the Lewis Chapter of the Daughters of the American Revolution thought it fitting to bestow the DAR Women in American History certificate and medal upon Ann Cole Lowe. A member of Lowe's family, Olivia Cole Welch (a cousin), received the award in memory and honor of Lowe during a ceremony held in Clayton at the City Hall in 2020.

Dothan Eagle, July 2020

In college newspapers…

"Remembering Ann Lowe, the Black designer who shaped socialite fashion

Praise for "society's best kept secret" of the 1900s on the 40th anniversary of her death

From The Cavalier Daily, Serving the University Community, Charlottesville, VA, February 2021

In Online Magazines...

New Yorker Magazine. Ann Lowe's Barrier-Breaking Mid-Century Couture   https://www.newyorker.com/magazine/2021/03/29/ann-lowes-barrier-breaking-mid-century-couture   by Judith Thurman

Brides: a DotDash epublished magazine. www.brides.com February 22, 2021 "Honoring Ann Lowe: The Talented Black Designer Behind Jackie Kennedy's Iconic Wedding Dress." By Maggie Kreienberg

Elle: www.elle.com September 12, 2019 "Ann Lowe is the Little-Known Black Couturier Who Designed Jackie Kennedy's Iconic Wedding Dress." By Rose Minutaglio

Princeton Magazine: http://www.princetonmagazine.com/an-uncredited-career/ "An Uncredited Career" By Anne Levin

Threads Magazine: Ann Cole Lowe, Profiles in Sewing History www.threadsmagazine.com/2021/02/09/profiles-in-sewing-part-1-ann-cole-lowe by Dana Finkle

On Television

Monte Durham of *Say, Yes to the Dress, Atlanta!* does not hide his enthusiasm for Jacqueline Bouvier Kennedy's style. He states that he considers her to be one of the most stylish women in history. In honor of Jackie, he has a replica of her dress in his home. You may follow Monte on his blogspot and podcast. The photo below shows Monte in his home with his replica.

Photo courtesy of Monte Durham.

As A Town Mural

Eight Alabama governors hail from Barbour County. Recently a Barbour County Governors' Trail Commission was established to promote tourism. They have proposed a town mural featuring the history of the town. One of the panels will feature Ann Cole Lowe. The artist has been selected and is ready to get started.

In Paper

This is a fascinating paper replica of Ann's design for Jacqueline Bouvier's wedding gown. Belgian artist Isabelle de Borchgrave, a prominent Belgian artist and sculptor known for colorful paintings and intricate paper sculptures was commissioned in 2004 by Chicago's Marshall Field's Department Store to create an exact paper replica of the gown. Mrs. De Borchgrave, along with her assistant, Rita Brown, visited the JFK Presidential Library and examined and measured the original gown.

Back in their studio the two women painted and prepared paper to mimic the gown's silk texture and color. The paper was then folded, glued and finally stitched. All elements of the original, the pleats, the circles, the florets, and the 24 inch waistline were replicated.

Today the paper replica can be seen at the JFK Presidential Library in Massachusetts.

Jacqueline Bouvier Kennedy's wedding gown in paper by Belgian artist and sculptor Isabelle de Borchgrave.

Permission to use photos courtesy of Isabelle de Borchgrave. Photos by Ghislain David de Lossy

Paper Dolls: Ann has also made it to paper dolls

Tom Tierney has
published an
assortment of
Jacqueline Kennedy's
fashions as a paper
doll collection.
Included in the
collection is the
wedding dress.

In Porcelain

The Ashton-Drake Galleries commissioned master Doll Artist Renata Jansen to handcraft a Diamond Anniversary Collector's edition in the finest bisque porcelain. Additionally, the Franklin Mint and Madam Alexander have both created porcelain dolls featuring Jacqueline Bouvier Kennedy wearing her Ann Lowe bridal gown. Here are two versions.

Porcelain doll from the author's collection

On the web (just a sampling)

Ann's fashions are captured in several sites. Often just the gown is shown, at other times a model or the owner of the gown is pictured wearing it. These photos can be found on numerous blogs, websites, and on pinterest. You will find more photos than I have included in this biography because many of the photographs are copyrighted and the bloggers and pinners do not have copyright permission. Since I have been unable to reach the owner of the copyright or the photo, I could not take a chance of using them in this written account. Do check them out to see more of Ann's designs.

Just as a word of caution, verify any information you find on these sites. Recently, I found a blog giving Ann's birthplace as Clayton, California rather than Clayton, Alabama. She was born in Alabama.

If I have inadvertently stepped on anyone's copyright photo, please let me know and it will be removed.

On the web from the author

Ann Lowe: 1898-1901 Something to Prove
http://fayeswordbasket.blogspot.com/2016/08/ann-lowe-1898-1981-
something-to-prove.html

What one strong woman with determination can achieve. Ann Lowe on
International Women's Day
http://fayeswordbasket.blogspot.com/2018/03/what-one-strong-
woman-with.html

Remembering Ann Lowe during African American History Month.
http://fayeswordbasket.blogspot.com/2017/02/remembering-ann-lowe-
during-african.html

For Indie Published Authors: Here's how it happened: My indie
published book to film option contract:
http://fayeswordbasket.blogspot.com/2017/12/so-heres-how-it-
happenedmy-indie.html

As a Podcast

https://www.seamwork.com/podcast/episodes/28

 Ann Lowe: Big Risks for Big Dreams

Related links from this episode:

Something to Prove, a biography of Ann Lowe by Julia Faye
Smith.
Faye's Word Basket, Julia's blog
1898-1981 – Ann Lowe, a short timeline article from FIT.
When Clothes Become Fashion: Curating the Museum at FIT,
an interview with guest Elizabeth Way in Seamwork
Magazine.
Fancy Party Gowns, a children's book on Ann Lowe.

On youtube

The Humanities Council of Washington D.C., presented a program
featuring Ann Lowe: Humanities Salon—Anne Lowe and the
BlackFashion and the BlackFashion Museum—in Washington D.C.:
https://www.youtube.com/watch?v=Jy92isc45sM

Pursuing hidden history in Delaware Margaret Powell
discusses Anne Lowe:

http://www.youtube.com/watch?v=CGkbHrEX14

In Museums...

Museums play an important part in any historical work of this kind. They preserve the past, share with the present, and preserve for the future. Ann's designs are enjoying a rebirth in many American museums. A sincere thank you to all museum staff members.

Museum Practices: Provenance

The history of ownership, or provenance, of a work of art represents one aspect of a complete catalogue record for any object entering a museum's permanent collection. Ideally the provenance would document an object's whereabouts from its maker to its present day owner, including all former owners, locations, and sale transactions. However, it is quite common for an object's provenance to have gaps, or periods of time where the provenance information is not known. Lack of information can result from any number of reasons; for example, a previous owner may have desired to be anonymous, or records were never kept.

It is because of the diligent work of museums around the world that the general public has access to works of art. The end products of fashion design, i.e. the gowns, dresses, suits, shoes, jewelry, etc, are pieces of the art world. As a fundamental part of its mission, a museum conducts research on works of art in its collection. An important part of that research is the effort to establish the provenance of each object in the museum collection. Often the artifact comes with identifying marks, such as signatures and labels. Still the museum with authenticate those obvious markings of creation. The objective of provenance research is to trace the ownership history and location of an object, when possible, from its creation to the present.

The four dresses in this work from the **Cincinnati Art Museum** (Ohio) exemplify this practice. The red-flowered dress is unlabeled, but the donor, the son of the woman who commissioned the dress, said that Lowe was the maker of the both the red-flowered dress and the blue-flowered dress. The detective work began.

Through the exhaustive work the museum, the field of red flowers once "attributed to" Ann Lowe can now, be identified as an Ann Lowe original.

A very special thank you to Cynthia Ameneus, Chief Curator, Cincinnati Art Museum and Rob Deslongchamps, Head of Photographic Services, Cincinnati Art Museum.

Museum Practices: Care and Conservation

The Textile Departments of museums specialize in the preservation of a wide range of fabric and fiber-based items which include tapestries, embroideries, flags, samplers, costumes, quilts, and weavings.

Most damage to textiles is age-related or from excessive use; over time, items may discolor, fade, darken, and deteriorate causing splits and losses in the material. Within a museum is a conservator whose mission it is to stabilize and help restore the textiles to near original condition. This is accomplished using delicate stitching and conservation mounting, and cleaning using appropriate methods and materials for the medium.

Reasons for restoration are many, most importantly to keep the items in shape for use within the home institution. Secondly, it is a common museum practice to loan acquisitions to another institution for special purposes. Recently Peabody Essex Museum in Salem, Massachusetts, asked to borrow an Ann Lowe cotillion gown from 1956 for a special exhibition. The gown was in storage at the Chicago Museum of History (CMH) and needed some restoration . The conservation team at CMH was asked to prepare the gown.

The CMH conservator and her team found that aside from age conditions and storage wrinkles and creases the gown was in fair condition. The damage that had occurred was largely from normal wear and had couple of missing or lose appliques and sparkles.

The gown, worn in December 1956 by Carole Duke Denham, for Passavant Cotillion in Chicago, is an elegant, flowing creation embellished with fabric appliques of long-stemmed roses, faux pearls, sequins, glass seed beads and rhinestones on the bone-lined bodice and down the sides of the skirt.

The photographs for this gown are under copyright and require a license purchase for use. The gown can be seen on the CMH site under Care and Conservation. It's an informative article.

Museum Technology:

At the Henry B. Plant Museum in Tampa, FL three of Ann's Gasparilla gowns have met today's technology. The Henry B. Plant Museum Society funded extensive conservation and detailed photography and scanning of the gowns. Using the scan, 3D models of the dresses were assembled. The one dimensional photography can be seen earlier in this work. You can view these gowns online at the following link thanks to the Museum Society. https://www.plantmuseum.com/exhibits/online-exhibits/gasparilla-gowns. Once you open the site use your mouse or trackpad to zoom in, rotate, and see some of the detail on the models of the gowns. Aging of photos may have impacted the color of the gowns.

Gasparilla Jewel Circle Gown 1957

Gasparilla 3 Eva 20190220 MA Final Low Res 300k by **plantmuseum** on **Sketchfab**

Gasparilla Jewel Circle Gown worn by Rebecca Davies Smith

(Mrs. Armin H. Smith, Jr.) 1957

Gasparilla Court Gown 1926

Gasparilla 2 300k by **plantmuseum** on **Sketchfab**
Gasparilla Court Gown worn by Katherine Broaddus (Mrs.

Archibald Livingston, Jr.) in 1926

Gasparilla Court Gown 1924

**Gasparilla 1 Eva 20190220 MA Final
300k** by **plantmuseum** on **Sketchfab**

Gasparilla Queen's Gown worn by Sara Lykes Keller (Mrs. W. Frank Hobbs) in 1924

Many thanks to the museums featuring Ann Lowe:

Durham Museum, Omaha, Nebraska
https://durhammuseum.org/

Cincinnati Art Museum
https://www.cincinnatiartmuseum.org

Henry Plant (Gasparilla) Museum, Tampa, Florida
https://www.plantmuseum.com/

Hillwood Estate Museum and Garden, Washington, DC
https://hillwoodmuseum.org

The John F. Kennedy Presidential Library and Museum, Boston, Massachusetts https://www.jfklibrary.org

The Metropolitan Museum of Art, New York City, N.Y.
https://www.metmuseum.org

Museum of the City of NYC https://www.mcny.org

The National First Ladies' Historical Site, Canton, Ohio
https://www.nps.gov/fila/index.htm

The Smithsonian Institution, Washington D.C.
https://www.si.edu/museums/natural-history-museum

National Museum of African American History, and Culture,
https://www.aia.org/showcases/6094129-smithsonian-national-museum-of-african-ame

Winterthur Museum, Garden and Library
https://www.winterthur.org/designer-ann-lowe/

Bibliography

Cabrera, Cloe. "For A First Lady of Style, It All Began in Tampa." Tampa Tribune, January 30, 2007." News article. Web.

Cheshire, Maxine. "Miss Lowe Puts Her Heart into This Wedding Dress." *Washington Post* [Washington D.C.] 21 May 1968. Print.

Congdon, Jr.,, Thomas B. "Ann Lowe: Society's Best-Kept Secret." *Saturday Evening Post* 12 Dec. 1966: 74-76. Print.

"1961 Aksarben Court." Telephone interview. Mar.-Apr. 2016.

Durham, Monte. "Celebrating a Bridal and Style Icon - TLC : Monte's Take." *'TLC : Monte's Take'* Web. 29 Mar. 2016.

Frye, Elizabeth. "Fairy Princess Gowns Created by Tampa Designer for Queens in Gasparilla Golden Age." *Tampa Tribune* 7 Feb. 1965: 6-E. Web. 14 Apr. 2016.

Gates, Jr., Henry Louis. "Black Slave Owners: Did They Exist?" *The Root*. Web. 14 Jan. 2016. <http://www.theroot.com/articles/history/2013/03/Black_slave_owners_did_they_exist.2.html>.

Gihvan, Robin. "Black Fashion Museum Collection Finds a Fine Home with Smithsonian." *The Washington Post* 23 May 2010. Print.

"1961 Aksarben Court." Telephone interview. Mar.-Apr. 2016.

"1961 Aksarben Court." E-mail interview. Mar.-Apr. 2016.

"Jacqueline Kennedy: From Wedding to the White House." *Ladies Home Journal* 1 Apr. 1961. Print.   A Look Into Her Private Picture Albums

Leslie, Patricia. "Washington Speaks." *: Vintage Gowns, Jewels, Accessories End at Hillwood Jan. 10.* N.p., n.d. Web. 2016.

Major, Gerri. "Dean of American Designers." *Ebony* Dec. 1966: 136-42. Print.

Miller, Rosemary E. *Threads of Time: The Fabric of History : Profiles of African American Dressmakers and Designers, 1850-2002.* 3rd ed. Washington, D.C.: T & S, 2006. Print.

Mulvaney, Jay. *Kennedy Weddings: A Family Album.* New York: St. Martin's, 1999. Print.

"Miss Anne Lowe Covers A Paris Fashion Opening for the New Age." *New York Age* [New York] 24 Sept. 1949: 13. Print.

"1961 Aksarben Court." Telephone interview. Mar.-Apr. 2016.

Pottker, Janice. *Janet and Jackie: The Story of a Mother and Her Daughter, Jacqueline Kennedy Onassis.* New York: St. Martin's, 2001. Print.

Powell, Margaret. *The Life and Work of Ann Lowe: Rediscovering "Society's Best-Kept Secret"* Thesis. Smithsonian Associates and the Corcoran College of Art and Design, 2012. Print.

Powell, Margaret. "ANN LOWE and the Intriguing Couture Tradition of Ak-Sar-Ben." *Nebraska History* 2014: 134-43. Print.

Smith, Ann S. "Ann Lowe: Couturier to the Rich and Famous." *Alabama Heritage* 1 June 1999: 6-15. Print.

"The Fashion Historian: Ann Lowe." *The Fashion Historian.* Web. 14 Jan. 2016.

Jennifer: "Delaware as Fashion Capital? A Story from Our Textile Collections." *This Morning Is History.* 2011. Web. 22 Jan. 2016. <https://thismorningishistory.wordpress.com/2011/10/28/delaware-as-fashion-capital-a-story-from-our-textile-collections

Tierney, Tom. *Jacqueline Kennedy Onassis: Paper Dolls.* Dover. Print.

Way, Elizabeth. "Elizabeth Keckly and Ann Lowe: Constructing Fashionable Black Identity." *Elizabeth Keckly and Ann Lowe: Constructing Fashionable BlackIdentity.* Web.

Wilson, Julee. "Ann Lowe: Black Fashion Designer Who Created Jacqueline Kennedy's Wedding Dress." *The Huffington Post* 5

Feb. 2013. Web. 15 Nov. 2015.

"Humanities Salon - Anne Lowe and the Black Fashion Museum." *YouTube*. YouTube. Web. 16 Mar. 2016.

"Pursuing Hidden History in Delaware." *YouTube*. YouTube. Web. 16 Mar. 2016.

Http://www.jfklibrary.org/JFK/Media-Gallery/The-Wedding-of-John-and-Jacqueline-Kennedy.aspx. Web. 12 Oct. 2015.

MLA formatting by BibMe.org.

PART VI
FROM THE AUTHOR

Inconsistencies…

Readers of non-fiction research based works will recognize inconsistencies exist. When the material presented is based upon first person interviews many years after the events occurred, one often gets discrepancies. At times, as others offer their memories of an event or person, that memory is colored by their feelings for the subject. At other times, even a typo in transmission can lead to an incorrect fact becoming part of the narrative. For these and other reasons, there are discrepancies found in Ann Lowe's story.

First and foremost is her age/ Ann's birth year has been quoted, even by Ann herself, as different years. It has been given as 1898, 1896, 1889, and even 1901.The year most often quoted is 1898. Late in her life she was quoting 1898 as her birth year. Suddenly then, there was a quote giving 1901. Was Ann being coy and trying to shave a few years off her age?

If 1898 is her actual year, then was she 12 years old and already married as one researcher believed based upon a 1910 census record for a small southern town near Clayton. That assertion has since been restated by others without further documentation.

Or, was she married in 1914, thus being a 16 year old bride as she herself stated in an interview? As often happens, one inconsistency leads to another. We have no birth records and no marriage documents recorded for her first marriage, thus this contradiction remains.

In today's writings about Ann there is a name change that came later in Ann's life and becomes a part of the inconsistencies surrounding her. Ann's first husband was Lee Cohen, and her son was Arthur Cohen, but somewhere along the line two future grandmothers of a child had a deep disagreement about that last name. Cohen was fine with part of the family, but the other part wanted to change it. So,

208

Cone was born as a surname for future generations. I'm finding that as more people write about Ann, they are dropping the Cohen altogether and giving, even Mr. Lee Cohen, the name of Lee Cone. Perhaps they're simply trying to avoid confusion, but I think it adds to it.

Another discrepancy is showing up based upon research by a respected researcher and fabric expert, but which she states clearly is a theory based upon people's thoughts, not facts. Still it is being quoted as fact by others. She states that she believe Mrs. Josephine Lee discovered Ann in a Dothan, Alabama department store rather than a Montgomery department store. She also expresses the belief that Ann was working as a stock girl and was not a customer when she and Mrs. Lee met. She believe this because 'that's the way it would have been back then.' Perhaps, perhaps not, but there is no documentation either way. Montgomery has long been quoted in this part of the story of Ann's life.

Inconsistencies arise also when two or three generations 'know' the story and it is considered factual, but through the years, these stories remain and become a part, often an integral part, of a person's biography. I've tried to research each salient point in Ann's life and believe I have presented her story, even with inconsistencies, as accurately as possibly.

The fact remains, even with discrepancies, that Ann was an amazing woman, one who should be remembered for all her brilliant talent and accomplishments.

Living with the vision of Ann

For the past six years, I've lived in the world of Ann Lowe. Through continued research, I've come to know this talented woman.. this fashion designer who designed for many but was known only to a select circle of clients because she was, in her own words, a "design snob." But she was, oh, so much more.

I met her in an airport in the fall of 1915. I was at the airport, she wasn't. She died decades ago, but as I was 'surfing the net' while waiting for my plane to be called, I came upon two sentences about her. A 'did you know' kind of post. I was blown away, for no, I didn't know and I thought the circumstances were such that I should.

Born in 1898, the great-granddaughter of a slave and a plantation owner, the granddaughter of a slave and a free man of color, she entered the world in a small, rural town in the Jim Crow South. Using her talent, determination, and a desire to reach a goal, she refused to let the circumstances of her birth keep her down. She didn't preach; she didn't march, she didn't give up. She allowed a dream to be born in her heart and in her own way, she overcame all obstacles and achieved her dream.

When I began my research, I was writing historical fiction. Soon it became clear to me that her story, her true, unvarnished story had to be told. It was, at that point, told only in bits and pieces and often with the bits inaccurate and the pieces changing with each retelling. I began my research to clarify things for myself and found myself getting to know a strong woman from a family of strong women.

As I researched, I gave up on the historical fiction for two reasons. First, her story in itself needs to be told. At times it reads rather like a fairy tale with its ups and downs and at all times is an inspiration. Secondly, I am a white woman, raised in the South. Try as I might I could not convince myself that I could do her justice in fiction. I could not get in her head and speak in her voice. I wanted her, through her decisions and actions, to speak for herself. I hope she does.

Along the way, I have learned to marvel at what Ann overcame, and

210

at the people she met. This woman who, at that time in history, under normal circumstances would not be welcomed in their homes, became a darling to the Duponts, Rothschilds, Rockefellers, Roosevelts, Lodges, Posts, Auchinclosses, the Bouviers,..well you get my drift.

As I researched her life, I found beautiful gowns and their owners. I have been in touch with some fascinating people; a lovely socialite who invited me to her home, the daughter of a novelist whose works became the story for several John Wayne movies, including the unforgettable, *Shane*, a former debutant who spent years in government service, and a lady who sounds like my mother-in-law on the phone.

I've wandered through graveyards, seen homes falling down, visited with ladies who still speak of the members of her family with their family nicknames as if they are just around the corner, and I've driven through beautiful rolling hills only to find an impoverished town at the end of the road.

Some will ask why, since she lived during the time of the Civil Rights movement, I did not include anything about her in regard to that. The answer is simple. I found nothing tying her directly to the movement. I'm sure she, like all of us who lived during those days, followed the events. I'm sure she grieved, as we did, with the deaths and destruction involved, but I never found evidence of her direct involvement. I think, in her own quiet way, she was cutting a path into the future for her race and her sex.

There are many years of her life undocumented here. Why? Again, because there are years for which I found no documentation. We know her big movements, her big achievements. Let's rejoice in those.

There is more financial documentation, but it all leads to the same end. Financial problems, tax problems, and bankruptcy. I wanted to celebrate her accomplishments. I'll leave the financial story to others.

For the story I've tried to tell of Ann, I hope I've told it well.

--Julia Faye Dockery Smith

Acknowledgements…

So many people helped me along the way as I wrote this book. First, thank you to Ann's Great-Granddaughter Clara C. Harvey who, representing her father, granted photo permissions and answered questions for me. To you both, thank you for sharing.

This book would not have been possible without the encouragement and support from Ann's lovely ladies. Heartfelt thanks to Ann Bellah Copeland, Phyllis Fonda Dahlke, Ann Jessop, Betty King, and Connie O'Neil. To the lovely Patricia Penrose Schieffer who generously gave of her time to gather and have reproduced the photos she shared with me, an immeasurable thank you. Thank you all for your beautiful photos and your memories.

A warm thank you to Judith Guile, Ann's former model. It was a pleasure hearing her soft British voice as she shared with me her memories of Ann.

To the helpful staff at the Henry Plant Museum in Tampa, FL and Hillwood Museum and Gardens in Washington DC., and Cincinnati Museum of Art, thank you for so willingly going out of your way and sharing with me. To the staffs of all the museums, newspapers, and magazines who took the time to go beyond their daily duties, thank you.

To Dr. Piper Huguley, author of the upcoming *By Design: the story of Ann Lowe, Society's Best-Kept Secret* a historical fiction of Ann's life. Expect publication in 2022.

To those who listened: Tricia Knox (*"Someone should make a movie of this,"*), Lorie Smith, (*"Great topic for a winning history fair project,"*), and to Paula Chambers and Terry LaSalle for always being my cheerleaders. Thanks to Lorie, also, for visiting the First Ladies' Library for me. Thanks to my Beta readers.

To my family, loving thanks for all your support. To my husband who lived through the research and writing of Ann's story, not once but twice and cheered me on daily, a loving thank you.

Finally, as always, thank you to skajejl for being my inspirations.

Books By Julia Faye Dockery Smith/Julia Faye Smith Available at Amazon, through ebook publiations, Independent bookstores, by order through big box book stores, especially BN, relevant museums.

The Only Gift: A story of early twentieth century abuse, survival, and a strong woman https://www.amazon.com/dp/B08K3P1LR2/ref=dp-kindle-redirect?_encoding=UTF8&btkr=1
Bridging Our Memories: A Rhys Harbor, Mature Second-Time-Around Love Story filled with music
https://www.amazon.com/Bridging-our-Memories-Harbor-Story-ebook/dp/B08JXNVW3F
Twilight of Memory: WWII historical fiction with the Tenth Mountain Division (America's Ski Troops)in trainin and in war. Colorado and Italy https://www.amazon.com/dp/B01D6FNN1I/ref=dp-kindle-redirect?_encoding=UTF8&btkr=1
Tommy: The Civil War Childhood of a President: The Southern Childhood of President Thomas Woodrow Wilson, a biography https://www.amazon.com/Tommy-Childhood-President-Woodrow-Learning/dp/1544163754/ref=sr_1
Something to Prove: A Biography of Ann Lowe, America's Forgotten Designer
https://www.amazon.com/Something-Prove-Biography-Forgotten-Photographs/dp/1532981333/ref=sr_1

The author invites you to view her author website at
http://www.fayeswordbasket.com
and her blog at http://www.fayeswordbasket.blogspot.com

To view the photos found in this book and more go to
http://www.pinterest.com/juliafsmith7/something-to-prove

You may reach her at anncolelowe@gmail.com or jfaye21@gmail.com

Reviews on Amazon, Goodreads, Twitter, blogspots are appreciated.

Made in the USA
Columbia, SC
08 November 2023

25669260R00128